Sailplaning

Creating a 4-D Life & Career

By Lorna Stalker & Liane Hambly

Illustrations by Liane Hambly

2023

Sailplaning Publishing

United Kingdom

ISBN: 978-1-3999-6493-7

Printed by J Thomson Colour Printers Limited

First published 2023

By Sailplaning Publishing, Kilmarnock, Ayrshire

© 2023 Lorna Stalker and Liane Hambly

The right of Lorna Stalker and Liane Hambly to be identified as the authors of this work has been asserted by them in accordance with sections 77 and 78 of the Copyright, Designs and Patents Act 1988.

All rights reserved. No part of this book may be reprinted or reproduced or utilised in any form or by any electronic, mechanical, or any other means, now known or hereafter invented, including photocopying and recording, or in any information storage or retrieval system, without permission in writing from the publishers.

Trademark notice: Product or corporate names may be trademarks or registered trademarks and are used only for identification and explanation without intent to infringe.

British Library Cataloguing in Publication Data

A catalogue record for this book is available from the British Library.

Names: Stalker, Lorna, author. | Hambly, Liane, author.

Title: Sailplaning, Creating a 4-D Life and Career / Lorna Stalker and Liane Hambly.

Illustrations: Liane Hambly, 2023.

Includes references and index.

Description: Ayrshire : Sailplaning Publishing, 2023.

Identifiers:

ISBN 9781399964937 (pbk)

ISBN 9781399968928 (ebook)

Subjects: Career Development | Career Coaching | Life Coaching

Printed and bound by J. Thomson Colour Printers Ltd, Glasgow, G5 8PB

From the Authors

<u>Lorna</u>:

There have been many days or moments in life when I have felt like a single feather, floating and tossed around at the mercy of the weather. When working and then writing with Liane I started to notice how many of these moments have shaped who I am today. Liane's humanity, gentleness, care, compassion and her vulnerability created an environment where I felt heard and valued.

<u>Liane</u>:

I'm one of those people who, in my waking life, often feels too busy to look up and be in the moment. Yet at night, in amidst my stress-related nightmares, I also have exhilarating and joyful dreams of being lifted by the wind and flying above the rooftops and forests. Working with Lorna has been a gift, a chance to do just that. I once told her that she had a weird mind – it was meant as a compliment, as the stories and connections she made took me to other places, other ways of seeing. We also laughed and shared. In the writing journey I made a good friend who helps me fly.

<u>Lorna & Liane</u>:

The eclectic bird on the book cover beautifully illustrates that we are each a collection of life experiences. We each need a nurturing environment to help us create and deepen the connection to what is important to us. Our hope is that this book provides you with an opportunity to reflect on what is important in your life and career. We hope that from this perspective the possibilities held for you within tomorrow, start to reveal themselves to you today, and that Sailplaning will help you figure out how to get there.

MENU

About the Authors — 6

How to use the book — 8

Ready to Lift Off? — 10
Please start by reading all 3 chapters
… then Sailplane to anywhere else in whatever order you like.
Sailplaning 11
The cannonball career 15
Did curiosity kill the cat? 20

Noticing … Yourself & Your Environment — 22
Yellow cars 23
Smart and successful? 26
Means of flight 31
Dream house 35

Vision, Inspiration & Courage — 39
The value of having dreams 40
Switch off your engine to daydream 45
Prescient people and positive dreams 49
The fear / desire see-saw 56

Self-Care — 62

The corner stone of myself – mattering	63
You don't have to do it!	70
Action and inaction (to go or to stop)	74
Can you … spot the difference?	81

Possibilities & Decisions — 87

I hope it rises	88
The pick 'n' mix isle	92
I like strawberries, do you?	98
Peeling the onion	103

Influences & Influencers — 106

Walls: boundaries, safety or confinement?	107
Who is driving your bus?	113
A high functioning crew	121
A basket of crabs or a pod of dolphins	127

Managing Your Career — 130

The river and the stepping stones	131
Distil your intent!	137
Tipping the SCALES … you're hired!	142
How to TACCL numbers	149

Glideslope into Sailplaning — 154

References — 159

About the Authors

"In a dream, I could feel the spread of my wings."

Lorna's Sailplaning Life and Career

A challenging childhood instilled the value of a strong family unit. As a wife, mother of 2, mother-in-law, grandmother of 4, sister, aunt and friend, Lorna has an established cornerstone on which she can depend, feels supported and able to spread her wings.

Lorna joined the Ayrshire Careers Service as an administrator in 1991. Following ill health, she was keen to add more building blocks, expanding her experience working with employers: labour market researcher, 'skillup' trainer, and then moving into roles supporting individuals: personal adviser, key worker, work coach, school careers adviser. Throughout, volunteering played an important role in stretching her skills: adviser, leader, mentor, teacher. Lifelong learning is at the heart of Lorna's professional journey, gaining qualifications in training, counselling, guidance, supervision, before qualifying with the MSc in Career Development.

This combined knowledge and experience supported her progression into team leader, then national operations executive, where Liane and Lorna connected to create a theory activity handbook for practitioners.

Liane's Sailplaning Life and Career

Growing up working class in South Wales, Liane was the first in her family to go to University. Frozen by a lack of self-confidence and a feeling of not being bright enough, she left with a top degree but unable to work out what to do next. She spent the next two years unemployed and struggling. The darkest times can be life changing experiences – insights into how hard it can be to navigate life and work decisions led Liane to a lifetime vocation in career counselling and coaching. She qualified as a careers adviser and initially worked in some of the most deprived areas in Leicester, supporting adults and young people to explore and have confidence in their potential. After a few secondments into training and research she eventually became a Senior lecturer in career development studies.

For the last 19 years she has run her own business – training, writing, coaching and supervising in career development. From frozen and being unable to express opinions at 18, she now delivers key-note presentations at international conferences. She believes that we are all in a process of becoming, finding who we are and taking our place in the world. Sometimes we need support from others to help, and writing this book with Lorna is something she hopes will provide inspiration and support to people on that journey.

How to use the book

Allow it to land. Pause, come back. Let deep shifts happen.

Metaphors and analogies

You'll notice pretty quickly that the book uses many metaphors and analogies. Why? Well, they are a powerful mechanism for burrowing deep into the part of the brain where limiting beliefs and habitual thinking lies and can unearth fresh perspectives and ways of being. Our rational, word-based brain is brilliant at analysis but not great at changing how we feel and think about ourselves. Those habits often lie in the automatic, feeling part of our brain which are gained through experience and stored in our long-term memory. Reason alone cannot penetrate those regions – we need sensory, experiential learning and life experience to create such shifts. When we use metaphors, analogies and imagination, the same bits of the brain light up during MRI brain scans, as if we were having that experience in the concrete world. It is the same as when we wake after a dream – our body feels as if it really happened (heart racing, feeling happy or unnerved). For these reasons this book seeks to harness the power of our imagination and engage our whole brain.

Imagination is a creative force that can unlock new ways of thinking. Some people refer to creativity as a noun "I am not creative", believing that it is something that you are. Creativity is best viewed as a verb, a skill that can be developed and improved. Whilst working through the chapters, you may need to pause, to sleep on what you've been thinking about. This will allow the creative and subjective part of your brain do its work before returning to the activity when the reflective and emotional dust has settled. You might find that the dust has turned into glitter.

Where to start?

Some books are meant to be read sequentially; this book offers a more curious approach - the opportunity to listen to yourself and see which chapters you are drawn to. Where you land within the book will depend on where you are within your life and career and what you wish to reflect on. This book is made up of seven themes, each with corresponding chapters. Their aim is to help you sailplane, to find and increase your sense of choice and influence over your life. The chapters are designed to use either independently or along with a teacher, career development practitioner, coach or friend.

The chapters throughout this book can be completed in any order, but the first Theme:

- ❖ Ready To Lift Off - consists of 3 chapters that provide a good foundation from which to sailplane. These chapters are:
    - Sailplaning
    - The Cannonball Career
    - Did Curiosity Kill The Cat?

There are 6 remaining themes all connected to sailplaning. These are:

- ❖ Noticing Yourself and Your Environment
- ❖ Hope, Inspiration and Vision
- ❖ Self-Care
- ❖ Decision Making
- ❖ Influences and Influencers
- ❖ Managing Your Career

The book closes with a final chapter:

- ❖ Glideslope into Sailplaning

Tools and techniques

Each chapter (with the exception of the final chapter) is similar in structure – theme introduction, narrative, activity and reflection. Some people think in pictures and some in words. Sailplaning activities draw on a range of tools and techniques, each designed to cater for different thinking styles. Look out for the following icons:

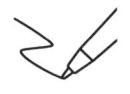    

Describe   **Draw**   **Cut and paste**   **Visualise**   **Model**

Career learning is for everyone - whether you are still at school, leaving education, transitioning from training into employment or self-initiating a change in your life, work and career. Individual chapters can be extracted and collated together to create a journal.

Ready to Lift Off

Chapter Titles: completing **all 3 of these chapters** will provide a good foundation from which to sailplane throughout the remaining 6 themes within the book.

Sailplaning

The metaphor of Sailplaning can work 4-dimensionally to help you visualise your career both now and in the future.

The cannonball career

What does career look and feel like in the 21st century? How does it look and feel like for you?

Did curiosity kill the cat?

Do we need to be more like a cat? Curious, knowing our lives can have many phases, walking away from what we don't like and trusting that whatever happens, in the long term, we will be ok.

Sailplaning

Imagine a bird soaring high in the sky. If a camera zoomed in and followed it closely, you would be able to see its head and eyes turning, looking from its unique perspective for something that only it is able to see.

Create what you are visualising (for example, what type of bird, how are the air currents moving?):

Describe   Draw   Cut and paste

Across the world birds have evolved to develop wings, perfect for their environment.

> From flightless **penguins** moving with great agility and speed through our oceans, to a **hummingbird** beating its wings more than 40 times a second, providing the illusion of floating at the entrance of brightly coloured, tubular flowers, to **gulls** with powerful flight feathers (called remiges) able to match the speed of many boats, whilst exhibiting very little motion across their wing span.

The 3 species of birds thrive in their natural habitat. But how would they respond if their habitat were to gradually change?

The changing nature of "Career"

In the 1980s and 1990s a logical career planning approach to structural transitions (for example, leaving education, retirement) was a tried and tested method and working well for many people. Before the close of the last millennia, post-modern theories began to alert the career development profession to a paradigm shift from linear career progression to individuals having a series of career decisions to navigate throughout their lifetime.

Generations of workers have witnessed economic and social changes that have progressively altered the traditional psychological contract between employers and workers i.e. there has been a gradual reduction of the long-term commitment of employers to their workers and vice versa. As this paradigm shift became embedded the labour market grew more unpredictable and career pathways increasingly unconventional.

To thrive in today's world of work, individuals need to evolve into active agents, skilled in managing their careers.

Sailplaning as a sport

Like a glider, a sailplane is an aircraft designed to fly without an engine and without the need for costly fuel. Unlike gliders, a sailplane is designed to sustain soaring flight by mimicking the long, broad wings of large birds, for example, gulls or storks.

At the turn of the 18th century gliding was a growing sport. It captured the interest of a young Robert Kronfeld who befriended Walter Georgii, a meteorologist who discovered thermals within rising air currents. By 1930, Squadron Leader Kronfeld had combined his experience as a champion glider with designing sailplanes. His knowledge of air wind currents, weather, terrains, as well as fuselage size, weight and surface area, allowed him to optimise his ability to soar. He set the world record for sailplaning at 164km and be the first person to make a return crossing over the English Channel.

Sailplaning is 4-D

The three primary dimensions are height, width, depth. The 4th dimension brings possibilities and imagination into play for example, a tesseract created within a cube (see an example on the back cover of the book).

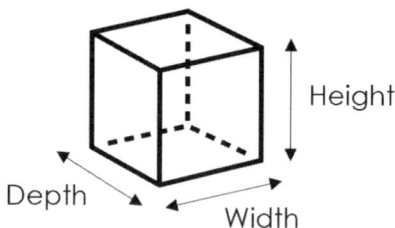

Take a few moments to look at your hands. They are 3-dimensional. Wiggle your fingers and roll your wrists around. You are now sensing their presence.

Visualise

Now imagine your hands doing something (you might want to close your eyes for this). What did you visualise? Were you playing music, shaking someone's hand, washing the dishes or texting a message?

Capture what you imagined:

Describe Draw Cut and paste

Visualising doing something with your hands is 4-dimensional - engaging your imagination and senses to move beyond 3-dimensions. The metaphor of Sailplaning can work 4-dimensionally by helping you to evaluate your present life and career and to visualise possibilities for your future.

There are 4 interconnected elements within Sailplaning (**SEA-C**):

Self: what matters to you is unique, complex and evolving.

Environment: you are part of a society and culture with spaces to learn and grow. Your physical and emotional sense of a place (belonging).

Abilities: you have cap-abilities (skills) which are innate, learned and developing. There may be poss-abilities you have yet to discover.

Connections: you have resources and relationships. These continue to build or re-construct as you encounter new experiences.

These 4 elements all contain a future focus, where visualising beyond today into tomorrow or next week, creates a sense of movement – Sailplaning.

Sailplaning is maintained adaptability, a state of being rather than a set place and time, when you are noticing what is happening all around you as well as sensing poss-abilities.

How are you Sailplaning today?

Here are examples - flying solo, riding a storm, soaring (strong), ascending (feeling good), flapping hard (to rise above a situation), spiralling (lost direction), circling (looking around but not seeing clearly), descending (slowing down).

On a separate page capture what you are visualising.

Describe   Draw   Cut and paste

Sailplaning can include all of these things.

You might be wondering whether your self-esteem, self-acceptance or self-efficacy are at the right levels; you may feel your wellbeing has been affected in some way and sailplaning is something you are not quite ready for. However ... if you:

- are able to reflect on your life and career,
- believe that there is potential for change and growth,
- feel ready to engage your agency and autonomy.

It is time for ... Sailplaning.

The following chapters will develop or refine your ability to Sailplane through currents which you may be experiencing or encounter in the future.

Erin's reflection upon this chapter:

"What I love about this chapter is its use of visualisation and imagery. You can use the activities to explore how your career journey could look and feel, or you could use them to support someone through this process.

This visual perspective will help you understand and gently explore what 'career' means today. Also, how career development practitioners can help you to open up your thoughts, ideas and support you navigate any challenges that may be anticipated. The important message of this chapter is how to tie together your - self, abilities and in particular your environment.

I loved the description of 'spaces to learn and grow', I believe this has the potential to inspire and nurture growth in everyone. I can't wait to use this explanation and the activities with the individuals I support."

Erin Bartley, Career Development Practitioner & PhD student.

The cannonball career

Decoupling 'Career'

Imagine the flight of a cannon ball. Shot from a stationary position by a sudden and deliberate change in force. The force of energy pushes it upwards through the air. It travels in a straight line away from the cannon due to the absence of air resistance and gravity. When gravity from Earth begins to act on the cannonball then it changes direction to a downwards descent. Velocity takes the cannonball towards the target. Where will it land - as intended on target, clip the edge, be a near miss, or be off target altogether?

Approaching the final years before leaving school, pupils can experience a build-up of pressure. Family and friends often ask future focused questions such as, "what are you going to do after you leave school". Young people can feel the need to select a career target based on varying degrees of belief or hope, before being propelled in a direction for a potential successful landing. This image is full of 'ifs', 'buts' and 'maybes'.

Until the 1980s, career was predominantly viewed as locking into a choice of one occupation, with formal learning and training anchored to early youth and early adulthood. In 1996 a book titled, The Career is Dead, Long Live the Career was published by D. T. Hall and Associates. The title inferred that that the world of work had changed.

Driven by increasingly unpredictable economic environments, organisations and individuals were progressively moving away from stable, linear career trajectories. Rather than feeling tossed about by the air currents, today's career works best when coupled with agency, that is, where you find and increase your sense of choice and influence over your life.

The agent

Agents are employed by athletes, producers, film, and media celebrities to represent their interests, build their career and validate their talent. In 1996, the movie Jerry Maguire, included the infamous line, "*show me the money*". It was the story of a sports agent who worked determinedly to represent the interests and build the career of one footballer, even when other clients had lost faith in Jerry's ability.

The philosophy of "agency" can be applied to the building of your career. When you create an inner contract with yourself, to value your talent and navigate the world of work by seeking opportunities to grow your career.

The sailplaning career

Individuals who consciously decouple their career aspirations from the traditional concept of career, view themselves as active agents – they no longer expect a linear trajectory into employment which ends in retirement. A sailplaning career involves a process of discovery where individuals draw on evolving skills, knowledge, and experiences to maintain career flight and soar above the landscape of a changeable labour market.

The images on the next page represent some of the ways we can view our career.

Which image feels familiar to your experience of career? What does the image represent to you? (image number and your notes): Describe
↪
Which image challenges or stretches your view of career? What does the image represent to you? (image number and your notes):
↪

These images may not fully capture your career, so you may want to create your own image of what career means to you.
Describe   Draw   Cut and paste

The modern career is connected to how you contribute to society throughout your life (paid or unpaid activities).

Write a list of activities / roles that you have experienced or expect to see within your career?
Describe

You may have mentioned school exams, training, college, university, employment. Other activities might include self-employment, volunteering, interests, hobbies, online learning, social media, gap year, travelling, caring.

Career fulfilment

Career fulfilment can feel like a distant target, the result of a long and straight trajectory. Conversely, if you view career fulfilment as a state which is achievable at <u>any</u> point in your life, even in the here and now, then your curiosity may be fuelled, driving decisions such as changing direction, stretching goals or continuing with the status quo. This attitudinal response changes the belief that career fulfilment can only be measured by success or failure later in life, into a recognition that career fulfilment is aligned to what feels like a personal achievement at any point in time.

Your Current Career Goal

Create a statement that captures feelings about what is important to you and any career goal that you might have:

Describe

It may be helpful to reflect on your statement with a friend, colleague, family member, teacher, or career development practitioner.

Jenn's reflection upon this chapter:

Reflecting on the imagery used in "The Cannonball Career" and the insights it provided, I couldn't help but visualise how I embarked on a career journey akin to sailing into uncharted waters - following what was 'expected' of a career at the time and, that was supposed to be linear, but ended up having many twists and turns. Like a cannonball changing trajectory due to unseen forces, my career path often felt uncertain (and still does at times). Like the image of the diverging road, I've had to make decisions at various forks in the road without knowing what lies ahead. The idea of signposts guiding these decisions and packing tools for this career exploration journey resonated deeply. However, the image of being stuck in traffic on a predetermined career path challenged my perception, highlighting the importance of individuality and spontaneity in seizing informed opportunities to divert off the "main route".

The hands-on activity of drawing my own career image tapped into my subconscious, allowing me to express my thoughts in a unique way. Listing future career activities encouraged future visioning and possibility thinking, emphasising how careers integrate into all aspects of life. Crafting a statement through self-reflection practice, about my current career goal reminded me of the significance of acknowledging feelings in this exploration process, blending rationality and emotion to develop self-clarity. In today's evolving world of work, I've come to realise that a sailplaning career, decoupled from traditional notions, empowers me to navigate the changing landscape actively.

Jenn Barfield, Career Development Practitioner

Did curiosity kill the cat?

The English proverb, "curiosity killed the cat" is meant to warn people of the dangers of being curious. It was coined in the 16th century and in fact didn't refer to curiosity at all, but to caring or worrying too much. Worry kills the cat, not curiosity. The other proverb, a "cat has nine lives" encourages us to be curious, to realise that the life we live is not just one phase, that we can move into other phases and live a different version of our life.

Cats are also very good at knowing what they like. Have you ever seen a cat having food put in front of it which it is not keen on? It walks away, goes through the cat flap of another house where there is better food and makes that its home.

The other belief often held about cats is that they land on their feet. So maybe we need to be more cat – be curious, know that our lives can have many phases, walk away from what we don't like and trust that whatever happens, in the long term we will be ok.

> What kind of cat are you today? Here are some examples: sleepy cat, hungry cat, hissy cat, scaredy cat …   agile, curious, brave, courageous, playful, adventurous, feisty (you can make up your own!).
>
> Choose a method to capture an image of your cat:
>
> Describe   Draw    Cut and paste

We are capable of behaving in a variety of ways, for one day or throughout a longer period of time.

What kind of cat <u>are you</u> the most often?   Describe   Draw   Cut and paste

What kind of cat <u>would you like to be</u> more often?

Vikki's reflections upon this chapter:

"During my career so far, I have worked in public and private sector organisations, as a teacher, recruiter, career development professional, performer, executive assistant and fruit and veg salesperson! I've also worked full time, part time, self-employed, freelance, on fixed term contracts and run a couple of side-hustles. On reflection, my ADHD-fuelled interest-based nervous system has gifted me curiosity in abundance and I have never felt afraid to try something new or, crucially, to stop doing something that is no longer the right fit for me. Some of my career pivots and job changes have been fully my choice, some have been less so, but a curious mindset has been key to finding the opportunity in the situation and turning it to my advantage.

You might be feeling like a scared cat at the moment, because you don't know what you want to do next? That's ok. The mantras of 'you don't know what you don't know' and 'you can't be what you can't see' is something that I have often encountered. I have also found that some people change their career goal when they learn new information about a job role. The key is to remain curious about what is important to you, what you like or don't like, so that you can seek out or avoid specific environments, tasks or styles of work. Become a curious cat rather than a scaredy cat about your life and your career, and I promise you'll be in for an interesting journey!"

Vikki Greary, Career Development Practitioner

Noticing Yourself and Your Environment

Chapter Titles: read the short statements and see which chapter(s) you are drawn to and sailplane from there.

Yellow cars

>Noticing what you are thinking, feeling and your motivations can increase your awareness of what you want to change or remain the same.

Smart and successful?

>We have different types of intelligences which challenge traditional narrow assumptions of what it means to be smart.

Means of flight

>Creating an aircraft to represents you, your personality, your hopes and dreams.

Dream House

>If you were to write a list of things that would create your dream house, it would be as unique as you.

Yellow cars

How often do you see a yellow car? Not very often! However, now this idea has been introduced to you, it is likely that you will start to notice yellow cars parked or driving past you.

The "Baader-Meinhof phenomenon" was used by Terry Mullen in a letter to the St. Paul Pioneer Press (1994) to rationalise why your awareness of something increases. Once you actively take notice of something, then you will notice it more often and probably believe that this is due to a higher frequency of occurrences. This is also referred to as frequency Illusion, a form of cognitive bias.

Noticing increases in frequency when the subject matter is important to you and feelings come into play. For example, wanting to start a family could lead to "there seems to be people with babies everywhere I look".

We can employ our ability to notice and increase awareness as a skill in decision making. Noticing what you are thinking, feeling and your motivations, can increase your awareness of what you want to change or remain the same.

Your drive ... guess how many yellow cars you will notice in one day. Pick a day and count them? Were you correct?

If you are in New York then yellow cars are a common site. So if you are not in New York when doing this activity, you can have bonus points if you see a yellow taxi!

A quest ... to understand what you are thinking, feeling and your motivations towards a task or situation.

Take 30 seconds to visualise a task or situation. Write 2 or more words against each points below, to capture your:

Describe

- Thoughts

- Feelings

- Motivations

Reflect on what you have captured against thoughts, feelings and motivations. Describe what you have noticed:

Describe

The skill of Noticing can be developed by allowing space to be in the moment and fully present with what is going on for you.

Picture a place where you are active (for example, work, study, volunteering, paid, or unpaid)

When you picture it, notice any sensations in your body, any feelings and passing thoughts.

What did you notice?

Describe **Draw** **Cut and paste**

Noticing and paying attention to why you have become aware of something, enhances your self-awareness. This activity can help you to reflect on your thoughts, feelings and then consider if there is anything that you would want to change.

Danielle's reflection upon this chapter:

"This chapter was relevant to me as a new student career development practitioner. I always considered myself to be an open and reflective person, however since starting the course I have noticed that my life and career, up until now, has contained many dimensions that I was previously unaware. A key feature has been noticing my ability to listen to both my thoughts and my feelings, so that the process of deciding what to do next is informed.

If you are at noticing that you want something different from your life and career, here are some questions that may help: what is important to you now, what makes you happy, what do you want to change, what do you *not* want in your life and who can help you?

The chapters throughout the book will ask you questions and encourage you to take time to reflect. Investing the time will allow you to gain confidence in your ability to make good decisions.

I think it is often helpful to pause and take notice of:

- what has happened?
- what is happening?
- what do you want to happen?"

Danielle Cipa, Student Career Development Practitioner

Smart and Successful?

What is "smart"?

"Stupid is, is stupid does" is a famous line repeated at various points in the movie Forrest Gump (1994). Each time this statement is used, it is in response to someone questioning Forrest's intelligence.

In school, pupils often measure their intelligence against standards meant to measure academic ability. If test scores are below average then the ownership of the 'I'm not smart' badge seems the most appropriate way to make sense of academic results.

BUT ... what is 'smart' and how is it measured?

Stupid   **M**ediocre   **A**verage   **R**emarkable   **T**alented

This range of words could be used to reflect how society measures 'smart'. However you could describe yourself as 'smart' against a broader range of measures, for example, you could be intelligent in your dealings with other people, in solving practical problems or in your relationship to nature.

Howard Gardner (1983; 2006) challenged traditional narrow assumptions about intelligence by proposing that people have different ways of being intelligent. The following activity is based on the work of Gardner and his multiple intelligences. Read through the list on the next page and tick all the things that you enjoy or are confident doing. There is an extra space at the end to add your own 'smart' option.

When is someone "successful"?

Success is a subjective measurement. Born from an individual's values and often influenced by society or culture.

Before local news coverage moved online, newspapers were filled with images that could be used to measure success, for example:

Homes / cars for sale	Holiday destinations	Job advertisements
Wedding photographs	Pictures of graduates	Birth announcements
New businesses opening	Sporting / musical accolades	

SMART OPTIONS	DESCRIPTION	Tick
Word Smart	Writing, reading, learning languages. e.g. Playing word games.	
Talking Smart	Telling stories, explaining things to others, e.g. debating with other people.	
Body Smart	Co-ordinating the body – creating shapes, responding quickly, e.g. dance, sport, acting.	
Maths Smart	Using numbers to solve problems, e.g. using graphs, timetables.	
Building Smart	Making connections using materials and tools, e.g. building a structure.	
Creative Smart	Generating new ideas or making things, e.g. crafts, designing.	
Space/ picture Smart	Visualising or seeing images in your mind, noticing and using space well, e.g. remembering images.	
Music Smart	Recognising tones, rhythms, hearing musical patterns, e.g. playing instruments or singing.	
Emotion Smart	Understanding people's feelings, intentions, motivations, and desires, e.g. showing concern and compassion.	
Spiritual Smart	The ability to contemplate topics relating to existence, e.g. interest or engagement in philosophy, spirituality and religion.	
Self Smart	The ability to understand yourself, to appreciate your feelings, fears and motivations, e.g. keeping a journal to reflect on experiences.	
Nature Smart	Sensitivity to nature, observing the changing seasons, feeling in tune with the outdoors, e.g. growing and taking care of plants.	
Animal Smart	Interacting with animals, understanding and caring for their needs, e.g. understanding different diets.	
Logic Smart	Using reason and step-by-step analysis to solve problems, e.g. following instructions.	

The "successful" newspaper images and messages presented various ways to measure your or another person's success. If you had a 'lovely' home, car, spouse, two children and a 'good' job, could afford an annual foreign holiday, then you ticked nearly all the boxes and the title of 'successful' could be yours.

Since the inception of social media, for example, Facebook, Instagram, Twitter, it has become easier to have a window into other people's lives. The window may provide a clear, unobstructed, real view of a life, or it may have been enhanced to control and project the ideal image (*see chapter: "Can you ... spot the difference"*).

Unsubscribing yourself from many of these constructed life values requires either a conscious decision to make alternative life choices, or it could be the result of circumstances outside your control.

Pause for one minute and reflect on this statement:

Success or failure does not equal self-worth.

Think about a recent time when you accomplished something that took slight or only <u>a little effort</u>:
   When was this?
   Where were you?
   Who were you with?
   What was the achievement?
   How long did it take you?

Visualise

Reflection: how did you feel after success which only took a little effort?

Describe

Now think of time when you accomplished something that took <u>a lot of effort</u>:
   When was this?
   Where were you?
   Who were you with?
   What was the achievement?
   How long did it take you?

Visualise

Reflection: how did you feel after success with a lot of effort?

Describe

Review both successes and describe any differences between how you felt?

Describe

Regularly applauding your successes large or small, builds self-worth based on <u>your own achievements</u>. This conscious action in turn, builds a positive view of yourself based on your intrinsic values.

For the next 7 days applaud every success you have achieved, large or small (you could actually pat yourself on the back). To help you remember, write them down:

Describe

1)

2)

3)

4)

5)

6)

7)

Alternatively, on a separate piece of paper: Draw   Cut and paste

At the end of the 7 days, reflect on your successes. Which ones made you smile the most?

Describe

Your quest ... to regularly find value in your own successes and to celebrate.

A thought: *uncoupling your self-worth from societal measurers of success or failure is easier when you celebrate successes that are unique to you.*

Jennifer's reflection upon this chapter:

"I absolutely loved the table about the different kind of smarts. This is a fantastic, confidence boosting exercise that gets you thinking about the different ways in which we can all be clever. This could easily be an activity for groups or to support career conversations with another person who wants to work on their 'self' area. It could also be an activity to gently help you increase your 'self-smart', combined with undertaking reflective activities throughout this book.

The section about success is great too. It's very important for people, especially young adults, to take a step back from success and truly reflect on what it means. The activity could be used in a discussion around creating a CV or personal statement asking questions such as Where were you? Who were you with? What was the achievement? How long did it take you? This will help to support people to write about their successes."

Jennifer Convery, Career Development Practitioner

Means of flight

When you were young did you ever try to mimic a bird? Maybe you tried jumping off a wall or sofa and flapping your arms as hard as you could, to see if you could slow down your descent back to earth? Lorna and Liane certainly did. It was disappointing to land with the same forceful thud!

It is well documented that throughout history and across cultures, people are fascinated by the flight of birds. One of the earliest ambitions to join these amazing creatures in flight is the Greek legend, Daedalus. You can probably guess what he did, even without Liane's brilliant image – he fastened feathers together to make himself wings.

Since 1903, when Wilbur and Orville Wright created and successfully flew the first powered airplane in North Carolina, aeronautical engineering has evolved into a worldwide industry which includes Aerospace Engineering. Each day across the UK, around 6,000 aircraft fly above our heads, but there are many other means of flight which humans have constructed.

Create a list of the different kinds of air craft that have existed throughout history, for example hot air balloon:

Describe **Draw** **Cut and paste**

Would you ever consider building your own aircraft? Some people construct an aircraft by following a specific design, others choose to purchase and assemble using a kit. There are however some people who design and build their own aircraft from scratch.

Imagine yourself in the combined roles of a designer, customer and pilot. You are going to build yourself an aircraft which represents you, your personality, your hopes and your dreams.

The environment for your flight
Think of a current challenge or situation that you are facing. Use this as inspiration for this visualisation activity.
Visualise

You may want to create what you are visualising on a separate piece of paper:

 Describe   Draw  Cut and paste

- Your flight ... height and/or distance, for example, across vast ocean or hovering above a town.

- The weather conditions and the effects of visibility, for example, calm, snowy.

- Imagine yourself looking down from the sky. What do you see?

Your next step is to design your aircraft.

Here are some examples. You might want to combine different elements into one aircraft:

Your aircraft

The 5 questions below will help build an image of your aircraft (on a separate piece of paper). It may be helpful to add labels to describe different functions on your aircraft.

 Describe Draw  Cut and paste

Choose an approach that will work for you:
- read all the questions and then draw your image, or
- read one question at a time. After each question add something to your image.

1. Which type or types of aircraft would represent you, your personality, hopes and dreams?
2. What is the purpose of your aircraft, for example, 'party time', 'to go boldly'?
3. How is the aircraft travelling (speed, pitch and balance)?
4. What is the age and condition of the aircraft, for example, is there anything damaged or is it in tip-top form)?
5. If you could change the aircraft (take anything away or add a design feature real, unique or imaginary), what alteration would you choose, for example, shield, viewing platform?

Your aircraft and the environment?

Look over what you captured earlier about <u>the environment for your flight</u> and then look at the image of <u>your aircraft</u>.

The next 5 questions can help you to reflect on how your aircraft flies:

1. How suitable is your aircraft for the conditions?
2. Is there anything that might put the flight of your aircraft in danger?
3. Who is in the aircraft (are you alone)?
4. Who would you like to have on board with you if anyone at all?
5. What are the roles of those on board?

When you were creating your aircraft for a successful flight, were there new insights into your current situation? For example, the activity may have raised a question around where you are heading and whether you feel equipped for what is ahead.

It is ok to stay with the not knowing for a while, to let any questions percolate. This can give time for your thoughts and feelings to connect.

Are there other areas that you could apply this metaphor to?

It may be helpful to discuss this activity with a friend or family member and/or visit the chapter "Prescient people and positive dreams".

Larry's reflection upon this chapter:

"If you are feeling stuck, grounded or that something is overshadowing the vision you have of your life and career, this chapter will give you a different perspective, a bird's eye view.

This chapter uses aircraft and flight as metaphors to explore where you are in terms of your career plans and your goals. I have heard a range of people introduce the metaphor of 'flight' into career conversations for example, progressing or embarking on a new experience can feel like 'taking flight', achievement is like 'flying high' and independence like 'spreading your wings'.

Noticing your environment, direction, pace of progress, how you are travelling, can help you to consider whether there are actions needed to aid a successful flight. The metaphors in this chapter can help you to reflect on your flight conditions, suitability of your aircraft and the journey itself, in relation to what you need to achieve your life and career goal(s)."

Larry Hansen, Career Development Practitioner

Dream house

A dream house (or home), is a place where all your needs are met, including needs that you might not know you have (until you move in). Your 'dream house' reflects your sense of style and the kind of life you want or don't want - relationships, location (urban or rural), children, hobbies, pets and work/life balance. If you were to write a list of things that would create <u>your dream</u> house, it is likely to be as unique as you are.

Capture the image of your dream house.

Describe   Draw   Cut and paste

What does this say about you and what's important to you?

A dream or a nightmare

Do you ever have dreams about a house or home? Not everyone can remember their dreams - if you are such a person, then you could engage with this chapter by choosing to daydream instead (the technique of daydreaming is described in the chapter *"Switch off your engine to daydream"*.

In psychology, dreaming of a house or home can be interpreted as representing you and your life situation. Recalling images and noticing the feelings they illicit can provide insight into what you are currently experiencing and even offer potential solutions.

Below are a range of common interpretations for aspects of house dreams. If they do not ring true for you then you may wish to treat them as mere prompts for reflection.

Building a house – what are you building or need to build in your life at the moment? How is it going?

Flood – is there something causing you to feel overwhelmed? Do you need to seek protection and guidance?

Buying – are you taking on or need to take on new responsibilities?

Broken house – is there unfinished business in some area of your life that you need to return to and complete?

Destroyed, demolished or collapsing – is there an aspect of your life that feels like it has or is falling apart? What do you need to cope with this?

Evicted or leaving – is there something (an old belief, habit or way of being) that no longer serves you and needs to be left behind?

Haunted – is there something from the past that is still disturbing you and invading your life.

Glimpsing new rooms – are there opportunities for growth that you could explore?

You may experience walking through different rooms that reflect different aspects of you and your life. Only you can work out what these rooms mean for you –

- Attic: storage, knowledge, the head.

- Basement: subconscious, forgotten, loneliness, experiences you'd like to bury.
- Kitchen: family, nourishment, stress, responsibility, temptation, business, activity.
- Bathroom: upset, relaxation, privacy, processing, cleansing, purging, stuckness, control, shame.
- Living room: family, community, social, relaxation.
- Bedroom: restoration, intimacy, rest, retreat, nurturing, security, nesting.
- Hallway: threshold, entrance, transition, protection, movement, liminal, interaction with outside world.

Transforming your dreams

If your reflections leave you feeling unsettled with a sense of something needing to change, then you can use your dreams to create deep shifts in the way you see yourself and your situation.

It is best to do this activity as soon as you wake up, so that it is still fresh in your mind:

- Close your eyes and re-enter the dream.
- Notice your feelings.
- Reflect on what the image means to you at the moment.

When you feel ready ...

- Make the physical changes within the dream, for example, rebuilding a wall, securing wobbly stairways, opening curtains to bring in light.

What if I don't dream of houses?

You can still use the method above even if your dreams don't include rooms and houses. If you are experiencing a challenging situation or decision,

- Imagine a room or house that captures the essence of this.
- Inhabit the space (using all your senses).
- Identify changes that you can introduce to make this space feel more positive.

- Visualise the changes occurring.
- Re-visit how the space feels.
- Repeat, introducing changes until the environment is right for you.

It might be helpful to ask someone to guide you through this visualisation or to share with them, what you have experienced?

Sabrina's reflections upon this chapter:

"While I'm not someone who typically remembers my dreams, I found writing out the answers to the initial questions very insightful. It is powerful to pause, be directed to go deep on some issues, and to do so in a symbolic way, such as with this house metaphor. I like how the authors equate "flooding" with overwhelm and "buying" with taking on new responsibilities, and my favourite is probably having the "leaving" tied to letting go of things that no longer serve you.

The question that I found the most interesting, however, was related to "destroy / collapse." We are being asked what aspects of our life have fallen apart, and then what do we need to cope with this? I thought that was a brilliant follow up question. I expected it to be, "how will you solve this problem" so it was very refreshing for it to be about how you will deal with it instead.

From this exercise, I was left with some reminders of things that I need to put energy into, a little bit more courage around some of my challenges, and the encouragement that we can build anew. There is power in getting these ideas out on paper and then beginning to imagine (in words or pictures) the transformed version, allowing those new phrases, or images to keep you buoyant during the journey."

Sabrina Woods, Holistic Career Coach & International Trainer / Speaker

Vision, Inspiration & Courage

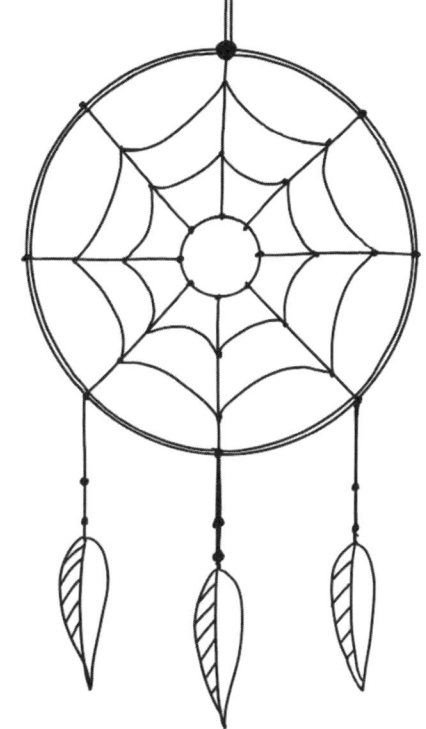

<u>Chapter Titles:</u>

The value of having dreams

> What would happen if everyone, regardless of age, were encouraged to visualise their 'dream career' in a field that fascinates them?

Switch off your engine to daydream

> Do you ever feel like your mind never stops? Even when you are still, you feel as if your mind remains on the go.

Prescient people and positive dreams

> A discerning or visionary person who usually dreams a lot *is* Prescient, able to hold a future focussed dream.

The fear / desire see-saw

> Fear can be measured in feelings of trepidation, on a scale from illogical to logical.

The value of having dreams

Dreams occur during REM sleep, when memories are consolidated.

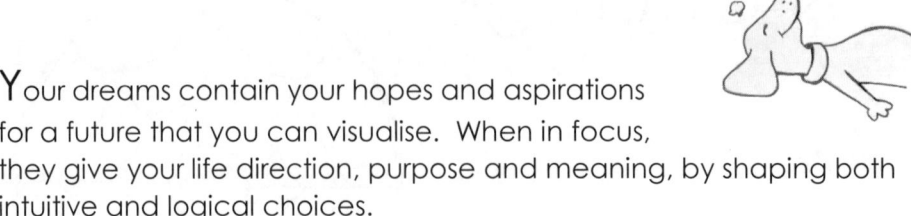

Your dreams contain your hopes and aspirations for a future that you can visualise. When in focus, they give your life direction, purpose and meaning, by shaping both intuitive and logical choices.

One of the world's most famous dreamers Dr Martin Luther King, as a child of 6 years old, had become aware of America's race problem. At 34, he shared his vision of a future, when everyone would be treated equally and employment opportunities were open for all. This captured the imagination of a generation and inspired societal change which continues today.

Inscribed on the steps of the Lincoln Memorial are the words:

> **I HAVE A DREAM**
>
> **MARTIN LUTHER KING, JR**
>
> THE MARCH ON WASHINGTON
>
> FOR JOBS AND FREEDOM
>
> AUGUST 28TH, 1963

One way to view your career is to identify how you can contribute to your community, society and the wider world.

What would you like your contribution to be? Capture your thoughts:

Describe   Draw   Cut and paste

What is a 'dream job'?

A 'dream job' is a manifestation of wants, desires and aspirations, culminating in personal visualisation of what success would look and feel like. It is informed by your experiences and constructs, up to that point in your life. Your 'dream job' can evolve and change, reflecting a growing collection of experiences and resulting in changing values.

It can be difficult for another person to see beyond the superficial factors of a 'dream job' and so it may be easily dismissed as a "pipe-dream" or unrealistic. For the holder of the dream, such dismissal can feel like a rejection of something that holds elements of their identity.

Children are often asked, "what do you want to be when you grow up?" This question encourages them to use their experience and imagination to come up with a career that makes sense to them at that point in their lives. Children find it easier to engage with the concept of a 'dream job'. However, throughout adolescence, influences and influencers may shrink the dream in favour of more 'realistic' options.

When a child of six years old, states that they want to become a superhero when they grow up, it can be interesting to ask them to tell you more about it and what has made them choose that role.

The role may reveal a value system that includes the desire to be brave, strong, important, special, save others, to stand up for what is right and wrong, to be a good person. Even if a dream seems unrealistic to an outsider, it can be symbolic of a person's values and identity and can be used as a vehicle to explore a whole range of thoughts and feelings.

Meet Liam:

As a child of six, Liam loved football. He grew up in a family who supported one of the 'big' Scottish teams. If you asked him, when he was little, "what is your dream job?", he would say "footballer". His parents provided lots of encouragement, his Dad even coached Liam's football team.

When the time came for Liam to leave school, he explored his choices with his family and careers adviser. Drawing the conclusion that a career as a professional footballer was not going to be possible, Liam used his organisational and IT skills to complete a Scottish Government administration apprenticeship. But Liam felt restless,

"life felt like it was happening in slow motion, rather than living my life".

Liam started exploring other ideas. With a Grandfather who had served in the Royal Navy, and with the Merchant Navy actively recruiting, Liam made a bold decision to leave a permanent position to re-train within an active and adventurous role. After Liam's Mum unexpectedly passed away, Liam was once again evaluating what was important and what he wanted from life. His mind was never far away from a football field. In fact his <u>field of fascination</u> remained professional football.

Liam's Mum's words, *"life is too short, take a risk and see how it goes, and if things don't work out, we can sort it"*, echoed in his mind. Liam was prompted to research careers within Scottish Football and completed football referee training at age 22. This re-ignited the passion for the dream.

A temporary position arose within the Scottish Football Association and he knew he had to take it. He wanted to test the dream - to see if it could work in reality. It was initially a 1-year contract, but the risk paid off. Liam could literally, on any given day, open a door to a football field and this became part of his career.

Soon he entered a full-time role which utilised his administration skills, supporting international youth football teams. Liam was very happy in this role, working every day within the sport he loved, travelling throughout Europe with people he had previously admired.

Unfortunately, his job became a casualty of Covid-19. Once again Liam researched related careers and was successful in his application for the post of a 'kit man' for a Scottish Professional Football League (SPFL) team. This role expanded his network and was where Liam developed a wider range of skills, both of which were key to being offered the position of football administrator with a Scottish Premiership team.

Throughout this journey Liam has developed career management skills which will help him navigate an unpredictable labour market, whilst still pursuing a career within Professional Football. Liam's story is far from finished... there could still be another amazing opportunity for him out there.

In Liam's words: "My career up until now hasn't been plane sailing, it's been more like Sailplaning. No decision I have ever made was the wrong one and every decision felt right at the time. I literally spent a month in the North Sea on rough waters, but I have also worked with people who have won the UEFA Champions League.

If my career in football finished tomorrow, I can always say that I have walked through the front doors of all the 'big Scottish teams' as part of a football team. I don't need to play on the football field as a footballer to live my dream."

Liam McDaid, Football Administrator, Scottish Premiership

 In memory of a special friend – Heather McDaid

Dare to dream

What would happen if everyone, regardless of age, were encouraged to visualise their 'dream career' in a field that fascinates them? Where might they land within a point on a spectrum of "greatly satisfied to greatly disappointed" adults?

Liam's story demonstrates that encouraging a "dream job" in a child or young person can result in an adult actively pursuing a career where they feel happy and fulfilled, even if it isn't in exactly the same shape initially imagined.

Your dream job ... when you were a child, what did you want to be when you grew up?

Describe

What did you **imagine** this job / role would involve?

What does this say about your **values** and what **fascinates you**?

↪

Your field of **fascination** ... describe or list what fascinates you?

↪

Ask yourself ... Are my current career goals or my career path in alignment with your values, interests and field of fasciation?

↪

Erin's reflection upon this chapter:

"You cannot underestimate the importance and mastery of this chapter. Career journeys are all about exploring and 'trying out' different options as Liam has done so far in his career. Testing and exploring allows us to learn and to develop our sense of 'self'. All of which highlights the importance of connecting life ambitions with career and how the use of a dream job (or job roles!) is essential when Sailplaning throughout your life and career.

This focus can be particularly helpful when working with adolescents, as this helps them to engage with their sense of 'self' and decision making as they develop and grow. This chapter sets out these concepts clearly and succinctly, with tips and activities to help you to reflect on your life. The concepts will also provide career development practitioners with techniques that will support individuals to dream, develop and grow."

Erin Bartley, Career Development Practitioner & PhD Student

Interesting fact: *We dream during REM sleep, when our brain is fully active, guzzling as much energy as when we're awake. REM sleep is ruled by* **the limbic system of the brain where feelings and intuition are held.**

Switch off your engine to daydream

Career decision making is often talked about as a thoughtful and rational process - where information is gathered, a range of options carefully considered and a logical answer reached . However, when making a decision about a future event when there is an element of uncertainty, reason alone is often insufficient – we need to also engage our intuition.

Pretz & Totz (2007) refer to intuition as a primary mode of perception, which operates within the human subconscious. Originating from deep within you and including memories that are both conscious and subconscious, intuition can be useful within career decision making (Abadie & Waroquier 2019; Dane et al 2012).

BUT...

Do you ever feel as if your mind never stops? Even when you are still, your mind remains on the go, running through lists of things that need your attention. You may even find yourself reaching for your phone or a scrap of paper (old school, I know), to note down things that you fear you might forget. Your conscious mind can feel like a car that, even when stationary, is idling.

Environmentalists encourage drivers to re-train their habits and turn off vehicle engines when stationary to avoid chemicals polluting the atmosphere. Idling is not just bad for the environment - it can also be harmful to your car (fuel may not combust properly, leaving residue that could be harmful for your exhaust), and for your health (poor air quality contributes to asthma, heart disease and lung cancer).

Switching off and on your vehicle's engine is easy, but switching off and on your thoughts can be a bit trickier, also involving elements of re-training and adjusting of habits.

So, what is the key to being able to switch off?

Sensing where you are

Listening to your intuitive self requires increased curiosity - noticing what you know, how you are feeling and what you are thinking. This does not need to be a complicated process and can be a simple as taking a moment to get a sense of where <u>you</u> are:

In the 1965 book about Bill Bradley, an American basketball superstar, McPhee guides the reader into the middle of the sporting action, appearing to draw on what Gladwell (2005) calls his adaptive unconscious to notice three things about himself:

1) He had extensive knowledge of the basketball game, so knew what good looked like.
2) He could visualise numerous highly skilled basketball manoeuvres.
3) He had feelings of astonishment at the level of skill being displayed.

McPhee witnessed something he had not seen before – Bradley was drawing on intuition to play across the whole basketball court at once, including making blind passes to team members and shooting without seeing the basket. Bradley demonstrated the ability to draw on his senses, to inform where he was.

Daydream

Daydreaming is often stigmatised as laziness, wasting time, or the inability to concentrate on a task. However, Daydreaming can also be described as a working or flow state when familiar tasks, for example, running, gardening, creative hobbies or reading, move your stress or self-doubt into the passenger seat and provides the opportunity for your body and mind to freely flow together.

Question - When was the last time you noticed yourself Daydreaming? Can you remember where your mind was taking you?

Introducing Daydreaming, without deliberately contemplating a specific task, could feel like stepping into an abyss, similar to a scene from the movie Indiana Jones and the Last Crusade (1989). Jones was faced with "a leap of faith". He had to take the first step, before the path (which had been there all along) could be discovered beneath his feet.

If you have not noticed yourself Daydreaming recently, take time now to pause <u>or</u> find some space within your day to take the step.

Below are some prompts to get you started:

1. Find a quite space.
2. Be still in your body.
3. Shhh & listen to your senses (what can you smell, sensations on your skin, the sounds around you, any tastes in your mouth, do you have feelings of tension and where are they within your body?)
4. Let your mind go on a journey and notice where it goes.
5. Feel in the moment (let any bad feelings go).
6. Explore, experiment and play with any pictures and words on your mind - look over the hill or under the water or finish those lyrics.
7. Reflect on whether your feelings have changed.
8. When you feel ready, stretch your body and gently move on with your day.

Daydreaming is a good time to ask yourself curious questions without the expectation of an immediate answer. Allowing the question to rest with you today, tomorrow or the next day, can start to develop your capacity to listen to your intuition.

When you are listening, it can be helpful to notice four things:
- What do you <u>Know</u>?
- What do you <u>Think</u> about?
- How do you <u>Feel</u>?
- Why do you think this is? (pull together what you are noticing).

Describe

Use this space to capture some notes:

It may be helpful to reflect on your thoughts with someone, although remember that your intuitive thoughts and responses are from your subconscious, so they are true to you.

Fiona's reflections upon this chapter:

"This chapter really resounded with me. Ever since I was a child, I have had such a strong belief in intuition, using it in every part of my life. As a career development practitioner, I use intuition to guide my interactions with the people I support.

Feeling the flow state as we daydream allows the conscious mind, with all its rules, fears and boundaries to lift away, revealing our true feelings and very often the decision that feels closest to what is important to us. Often our minds can feel cluttered and it can be challenging to find that moment to switch off the engine and daydream - it feels like an indulgence and perhaps a childish one. I love that this chapter reflects on the health and environmental benefits of switching off the car engine. Just as when we switch off our car engine, switching off our thinking engine to daydream allows a stillness where the pure, fresh air of our deepest feelings can flow freely. In the stillness we notice our bodies, our breath, noises which had gone unnoticed, and allow our imaginations to explore other realms of possibility.

Switching off your engine to daydream could help you to feel calmer and more engaged, but also sense the right decisions and dream bigger."

Fiona Athron, Career Development Practitioner

Prescient people and positive dreams

The term for a discerning or visionary person who dreams a lot *is* Prescient. Often met by scepticism in other people, a prescient is able to hold a future-focused dream.

Dream catchers originated within Native American Culture. Created using a willow hoop, web netting and decorated with sacred items, for example, feathers, dream catchers were hung outside the home in a window or courtyard area, to catch bad dreams and let positive energy through.

Two prescient individuals who drew on positive energy and held their future focused dream when faced with adversity were:

Walt Disney – in his early career Walt was told that his cartoons were not creative enough. Nonetheless, he held onto his dream and eventually created the Walt Disney Studios and led the world of animation. Today, The Walt Disney Company is described as a worldwide, mass media and entertainment conglomerate.

Henry Ford – in his early career, five of his companies bankrupted and he may have given in. Yet he held onto his dream and went on to become founder of the Ford Motor Company. As Chief Developer of the assembly line, Ford changed production practices enabling the mass production of affordable automobiles. These production practices influenced assembly lines throughout many industries.

Both individuals held onto a future-focus. When faced with obstacles, disappointment or even failure, they drew on their resilience, and were fuelled by hope and a vision of a successful future. There was pure alignment between their needs and wants - they were therefore Sailplaning through their career.

We all hold within our thoughts and feelings a range of unique wants and needs.

> ➢ Needs are what we feel we cannot do without to sustain the status quo. Your needs can change whenever the status quo is confronted by planned or unexpected events. Examples of

needs include survival, security, belonging, purpose and fulfilment.

> Wants are choices, desires or aspirations, which provide the motivation to bring about change. Sometimes we can feel confused because other people's expectations or pressures can cloud the integrity of our vision. When your vision is pure it is easier to set goals.

Actively listening to your 'self', can activate an alignment between our wants and needs. There are times when we experience an alignment, for example, when we have enough money (a need) to buy something we want. However we may experience times when our physical wants and needs are in conflict, for example, spending (want) and budgeting (need). There may also be times when our psychological and emotional wants and needs are misaligned, for example status (want) and creativity (need).

This chapter can support you to sailplane through times when your wants and needs are misaligned. Noticing a time of conflict provides the opportunity to create a "change environment", a place and period to ponder, listen and envision. To readjust what is required to create alignment.

ENVISION – becoming prescient!

Use this activity to release your prescience.

A) Ponder: 'what is important within my life and career?' What feels right or is it clouded by expectations?

B) Set yourself a period of time (the following activity is for 3 days, but you can decide on the length).

C) Each day, complete the statements. Distinguishing between needs and wants can be challenging as we often confuse the two. Returning to the definitions and talking it through with a career development practitioner or another person may help.

Take a note of your responses each day:

Day 1
- I need …

- I want …

- Reflect on what the statements say about you and/or your current thoughts, feelings and situation?

Day 2
- I need …

- I want …

- Reflect on what the statements say about you and/or your current thoughts, feelings and situation?

Day 3

> I need …

> I want …

> Reflect on what the statements say about you and/or your current thoughts, feelings and situation?

D) At the end of the set time period, take time to reflect on all of your statements, maybe with someone who is a 'good listener'.

What do you 'notice'? Are there patterns within:
> Your feelings
> Your thoughts
> Your self-talk

E) The next step is to ENVISION a future where your needs and wants are aligned.

Use the dream catcher (*on the next page*) to capture your <u>positive</u> dream. Divide the area (similar to a web) to create different sized spaces, to reflect their importance. In each section capture images of your envisioned future.

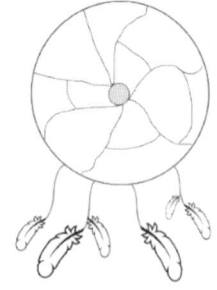

Describe

Draw

Cut and paste

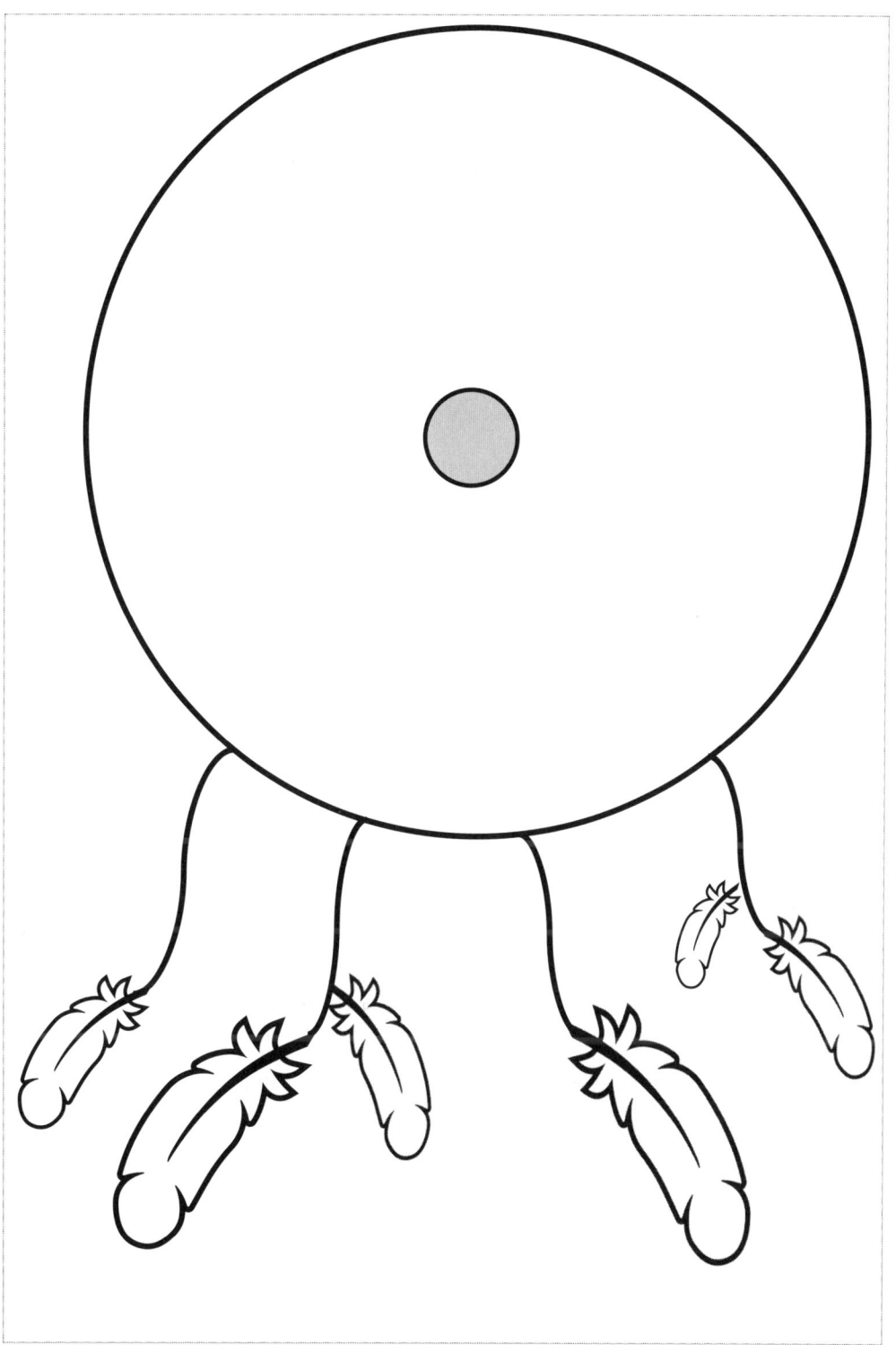

F) The last step is to decide on a goal and consider what to do next.

I will …   I can …   I am …   **Describe**

Start your goal and any actions with one of these 3.
In doing so, you are encouraging positivity.

Goal

→

Actions

→

→

Weakening self-doubt

Taking time to connect with your 'self', may bring into focus some negative feelings but don't try to squash them - today, they are part of you. Let them Sailplane with you, until their hold weakens.

One day you will feel able to let them go - that day may be today, tomorrow or next year. Until that day … continue to Dream.

Heather's reflections upon this chapter

"When reading this chapter, it led me to remember that I had an overwhelming 'need' to achieve dizzying heights of success, within an industry I thought was hard wired into my psyche, not just driven by me but also by other people's expectations. This masked expectation was a familial driver, meandering its way through many previous generations and found me waiting and wanting. I had attached my need to succeed to this runaway stagecoach, which then hurtled its way through dangerous and often heart stopping financial gullies and peaks of adrenaline. It eventually came to an abrupt halt, when I accepted that I was not able to sustain, never mind achieve, what I thought I wanted.

Over some time and after many conversations with myself, disappointment at my failure and late-night angst over my old dreams and nightmares, were swept up by dream catchers and dissolved into the ether. This created space for me to return to my love of understanding others, their drivers, dreams and helping them achieve those.

In reflection, I can see that I experienced a variety of massive peaks and troughs, however I am glad that I took the path that I did, because it led me to where 'I wanted to be' - eventually."

Heather Cipa, Career Development Practitioner

The fear / desire see-saw

Similar to 'dreams', fear has forward looking focus, coupled with an apprehension that something bad will happen. Fear is learned behaviour, constructed from all kinds of experiences. We all need to experience fear as it guides us away from danger or changes that can be life threatening or cause unhappiness.

Fear can be measured in feelings of trepidation, on a scale from illogical to logical. Very young children are taught by their families about legitimate dangers but they can also learn unnecessary fears, for example, that of spiders (unless you live in Australia!).

Which of these three characters (Scarecrow, Tinman or Lion) from The Wonderful Wizard of Oz (L. Frank Baum, 1900), experienced fear?

The answer is that all three characters experienced fear, but only the Lion initially focused on everything he was afraid of.

Lion - "Look at the circles under my eyes, I haven't slept in weeks."

Tin Man – "Why don't you try counting sheep?"

Lion – "That doesn't do any good, I'm afraid of them"

The Wizard of Oz (MGM Studios, 1939)

Alone, the Lion struggled to manage his fears. He believed that the Wizard would fix this by giving him the courage he needed. However, his new friends (Dorothy, Scarecrow and Tin Man) challenged and supported him, unlocking the inspiration and motivation he needed to face his fears. Towards the end of the story, the curtain was pulled back to reveal <u>not</u> a Wizard, but an ordinary man with no magic wand. The Lion had to find the answer within himself, made easier by the courage he had found on the journey. He was then awarded a medal for his courage - The least courageous became the most courageous.

When faced with career uncertainty or during a period of transition (planned, forced or self-initiated), you may become fearful with negative thoughts preventing you from seeing a way forward. Naturally, we want someone to "fix it" and tell us what to do, but when the curtain is pulled back, an ordinary person without the answers and magic wand is revealed. We can be left feeling frustrated or disappointed.

Drawing on your own resources is ultimately better. Finding these resources requires a different perspective of the situation but this can be hard to achieve on your own. Good companions on the journey (wise and compassionate) may challenge you to think differently and support you to take action. Who do you have, that could fulfil the role of a wise and compassionate companion?

List the people who help you to think differently, to explore fresh perspectives?

Describe

Do the same people support you to take action or are there others who can help with this? If so, list them here.

Alternatively, research ways to engage with local or national career services (helplines, college, school, careers centres). Write down any details below:

Describe

Read the story below to discover the scaffolding which can be used to design a strategy for managing fear. <u>Notice</u> the words in '**bold**', these will be used when writing your own story.

I have an illogical fear of worms. I know it is **illogical**, but just the thought of worms can lead to an actual shiver down my spine. As a young child I used to play in garden soil, happily handling the worms. However when my older sister, with great drama and gusto said, "Watch out for the thick red worms, they want to suck your blood. Look here", pointing at a worm wiggling near my foot, "that's why they are red". I jumped away in instant fear and from that moment it all changed. I had no reason to **question** her statement, after all she was 4 years my senior and knew a lot more than me, about all sorts of things. The fear was compounded during my 1st year in high school, when I was told by a science teacher that I must handle worms in order to complete an experiment. I tried to explain that I was genuinely frightened, but the teacher insisted, unable to see any logic behind my protests.

As an adult, my regular worm **avoidance behaviour** worked for me in many situations, often to the bemusement of people in my company. However a few years ago, when I moved to a new house with a large overgrown garden, I became aware that my worm avoidance behaviour was **no longer working** for me. My fear had become a barrier, blocking **my desire** to use gardening as a form of exercise and to be creative including growing my own vegetables.

My feelings see-sawed between fear and desire. I had to weigh-up **pros and cons**, what to do, or not to do. I started to **visualise a different scenario**, I could imagine what the garden would look like (I always wanted to keep ducks) and as a child I remember picking blackcurrant's for jam and eating fresh, warm, buttered potatoes, all products from family gardens.

My desire to create a working garden grew, eventually **tipping the balance.** The fear did not magically disappear, but I was motivated to find **approaches** to manage feelings that often resulted in me fleeing from the scene. I created a mental 2-point **action plan**: 1) research - speaking with people, 2) informal online learning.

I found out that hens, rather than ducks would clear and maintain one area, keeping weeds and bugs at bay with fresh eggs as a bonus. The second area was down to me. I bought myself long handled **tools** to keep me as far away from the soil and worms as possible. On occasions I stepped away, taking time out to talk myself through the fear before I was able to return to working with the soil.

I still experience fear of worms, regardless of how helpful they are for the garden. But the desire for a working garden eventually outweighed the fear.

A strategy for fear
Illogical
Question
Avoidance behaviour
No longer working
My desire
Pros and cons
Visualise a different scenario
Tipping the balance
Approaches
Action plan
Tools

<u>Are you curious about a strategy that could work for you?</u>

If so, take a few minutes to think about what causes you to experience fear that stops you from exploring possibilities or pursuing a dream.

Build your story by answering the scaffolding questions:

- What is my **illogical** fear?
- **Question** what caused me to be afraid?
- What is my **avoidance behaviour**?
- When and why is this behaviour **no longer working**?
- What is **my desire**?
- What are the **pros and cons** for bringing about change?
- What helps me **visualise a different scenario**?
- What is **tipping the balance** towards me needing to change?
- Which **approaches** could I use?
- What would I put in my **action plan**?
- What **tools** do I have or need?

Your story:

Describe

Jen's reflections upon this chapter:

"Fear has the ability to steal your joy. Sometimes your thoughts don't serve you and it takes awareness, time and effort to use metacognition and reflection, to identify and evaluate those illogical thoughts. Then to put scaffolding in place to reframe your mindset and support you to move forward.

I absolutely LOVE the see-saw analogy and the idea of 'tipping the balance' instead of focusing on conquering fear. When I was reflecting on the scaffolding questions, I could hear questions that I constantly ask myself and are really helpful – 'What is the evidence that this thought is true?' or 'What is the evidence that this is something to be afraid of?' In my day-to-day life I consistently encounter feelings of fear, however focusing on my desire, reminding myself that thoughts are not facts and having strategies in place that help me feel safe and outweighs my fear. It was so lovely to see this chapter reflect my experience of constructing my career journey.

I loved the positive outlook on fear and how fear helps us to survive. The world of work is unpredictable and many of us are likely to experience multiple transitions throughout our journey. The challenge is to be comfortable being uncomfortable, to continue as a lifelong learner and regularly stretch ourselves.

It is important to have someone else support you, to challenge your thinking. As career development practitioners we support individuals to reflect on what might be holding them back. We hear their fears and we use our questioning techniques to explore their thinking and encourage self-reflection. For some individuals, fear is rooted in trauma and the journey towards healing could take years, impacting on career development. However career development practitioners can nurture a positive mindset by supporting each person to identify unique goals and actions."

Jen O'Donnell, Career Development Practitioner & Education Executive

 In memory of an influential friend – Wendy (MacDonald) Smith

Self – care

Chapter Titles: read the short statements and see which chapter(s) you are drawn to and sailplane from there.

The corner stone of myself – mattering

The corner stone is often regarded as the most important part of a building and serves as the reference point for laying all the other stones.

You don't have to do it!

Are you being your genuine self? What do you most enjoy spending time doing? Which elements may increase your career happiness?

Action and inaction (to go or to stop)

Are you feeling ambivalent about taking action, or feel motivated but don't know where to start?

Can you … spot the difference

Your self-image influences your actions, which in turn impacts the decisions you make throughout your life and career.

The corner stone of myself – mattering

The corner stone is often regarded as the most important part of a building – it is a large stone at the base and serves as the reference point for laying all the other stones. Imagine that the building is your "self". In careers work we consider the building blocks of "self" as our interests, strengths, values, abilities, qualities. But what about the cornerstone of self-worth? Self-worth is related to but subtly different from self-esteem and confidence in that it isn't linked to achievements or other external reference points. Self-worth is a sense that I have value as a human being, even when I don't achieve, when things fall apart, or when I disappoint others. It is a kindness, compassion and gentleness towards one's self in full awareness of "failings", not a state of denial but one of full awareness and acceptance. It is the cornerstone of confidence, esteem, resilience and courage.

We need to know that we matter; we need to have a sense of our worth and value in order to take our place in the world. Without self-worth, we may not feel good enough, feel hopeless and demotivated; we may struggle to believe that our actions make any difference or that anyone cares; a self-critic hovers over everything we do, pulling it apart until we have reinforced our negative beliefs. Even when there is rational evidence of achievement such as qualifications and positive feedback from others, imposter syndrome sneaks in to discredit and undermine.

What's this got to do with my career?

Someone who has a healthy sense of self-worth will:

- apply for jobs for which they have the potential but may not have all the experience and skills in the specification,
- ask for a salary that reflects their worth,
- make sure they have a good work-life balance,
- say "no" to unrealistic demands,

- avoid burn-out,
- accept constructive criticism with grace and seek to learn from it,
- accept praise and gratitude with grace,
- manage stress effectively.

Here's an example – **Jas' story**

Jas applied for thirty jobs until they were successful – during that time they sought advice on their application skills and reminded themselves that the competition was tough and not to take rejection personally. Jas was quite happy in the role until a new manager came and started to micro-manage. For a while the continuous scrutiny led Jas to double-check their work and feel stressed. Then Jas thought "hang on, I can't keep going on like this or I'll get ill". Jas knew they either had to sort things out with their boss or find a new job. Jas tried to have a conversation with the manager but could see that it wasn't going to work, so they resolved to find a new job, one where they felt they could be creative and autonomous. In the meantime, Jas focused on keeping their boundaries with the manager and making sure they didn't take work home. They made sure the work was of a good enough standard but to keep everything in perspective. Outside of work Jas concentrated on looking after their health and well-being, which for Jas was walking in nature, seeing friends and eating well.

Jas's self-worth is pretty solid. Sometimes it is at risk of being undermined, but Jas notices and takes action. They have perspective on situations, taking responsibility but also maintaining boundaries with others. Jas works on what is within their control and avoids becoming bogged down with what they can't change, either about the situation or other people.

How solid is my cornerstone?

Some people might have high self-worth due to their early experiences – others may have a smaller cornerstone due to theirs. Whatever the size, it's important to nurture what you have. Signs that your self-worth is being undermined may include:

- looking at job descriptions and focusing on what you can't do rather than what you can,
- lack of assertiveness in meetings, letting other people steal your ideas without protesting, not negotiating a salary as good as that your peers are on,

- your mood dipping if you receive the slightest bit of criticism,
- your mood dipping if your social media messages haven't been acknowledged or liked,
- comparing your grades, achievements, salary, career, looks, etc with those of other people and feeling that somehow, you're not as good,
- continually criticising what you've said and done, going over and over it in your mind,
- feelings of failure, focusing on your "mistakes" much more than you do your achievements,
- imposter syndrome – feeling that other people will find out that you're not as good as they think and that you'll not meet up to expectations,
- late at night, when trying to sleep, your mind revisiting the day and thinking of what you should or could have done differently,
- perfectionism – only thinking you are good enough if you achieve 100%.

Reflection:

"I matter"…	"I do not matter"…
	Describe
What colour captures feelings within the statement "I matter"?	What colour captures feelings within the statement "I do not matter"?
Describe the colour:	Describe the colour:
How do I behave when I feel that "I matter"?	How do I behave when I feel that "I do not matter" …

Protecting your self-worth

There are actions we can take, habits we can break, to protect our self-worth.

Communicating

Being clear with other people about what matters to you, for example, your pronouns. They cannot respect what matters to you if they do not know.

Pause – identify – prioritise

This is a stress management technique that may help to protect your self-worth. Jas notices that they are getting stressed and pauses ("hang on ..."), identifies that double-checking their own work due to anxiety of being criticised and found wanting, was making them stressed (identify the problem). Jas prioritised their wellbeing (not burning out) as more important than pleasing their boss, and then thought of potential action to take.

The following template is something you can use when you start to notice that you are not protecting your self-worth.

Describe

Situation ….	
Notice What are the signs that I'm not looking after myself, for example, anxiety, tight jaw, knot in stomach, distracted, tired, eating or drinking the wrong things?	What are your signs?
Pause Find a way of not reacting – maybe breath, sit down with a cuppa, take a walk and …	How will you pause?

| Identify
What's causing this? Ask yourself if you are allowing your self-worth to be compromised in any way and what the reason is?	What's going on?
Prioritise:
Actively decide to protect your self-worth. There might be some discomfort, for example, guilt or anxiety. Ask yourself "what's the worst that can happen if I do this?" and see if you can live with the consequences.	What action, no matter how small, can you take to protect your worth?

Remember that if you do not look after the cornerstone then you will be of no use to anyone else.

Detachment and perspective

Jas applies for thirty jobs before they are successful. We're not talking being in denial and avoiding constructive feedback – Jas seeks out feedback and takes it on board. They are also able to stand back and keep perspective, to work out what is within their control and what has nothing to do with them.

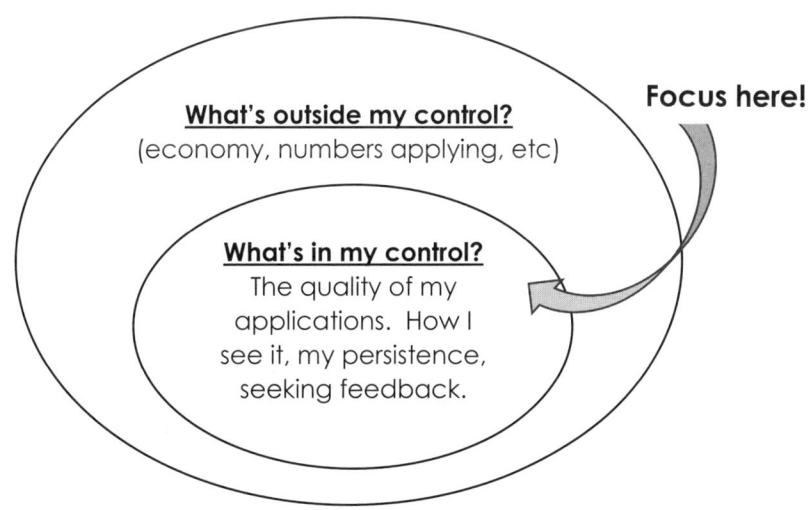

Not taking things personally still requires self-awareness and responsibility, to recognise your part (owning your stuff) and also being able to spot when someone's reactions, emotions or behaviour isn't to do with you - that they have their own stuff going on.

How to do this? Try the helicopter position – use your imagination to zoom out and look at what's going on from a distance.

Reflect on what is going on for you but also what could be going on for them. You may even feel a degree of compassion, for example, Jas might think the boss could be anxious about losing control. This isn't about rescuing the person, but having insight and compassion will allow you to take a step back, detach and move forward.

Me	Them
What's going on for me? Is this a habitual response of mine? Is there some experience from my past that is making my response heightened? Are my thoughts helping or hindering?	What could be going on for them that has nothing to do with me? How are they used to people responding to their behaviour? If I behave as expected, what are the consequences for me but also for them (what will it confirm)?
Describe	

Having self-worth helps you to be happy and fulfilled in your life and career but it can be undermined and we have to work at maintaining it.

Professional help:

If you believe that your lack of self-worth is deep, then you may consider support from a mental health practitioner. Talking from personal experience (Liane here!) each person's journey towards full mental health is very unique and what works for one person doesn't for another. I have a medical diagnosis of chronic lack of self-worth and have lived with it for 30 years. I've tried a range of approaches including therapy, exercise, medication, alternative health methods, reading a pile of self-help books, spirituality and diet. I won't say what works best for me as it might be different for you, but I have found a way of living creatively with my demons. Initially I thought I should be able to do it by myself, but other people's support and expertise has been invaluable on the way.

Shayla's reflections upon this chapter:

"This chapter resonates with me on so many levels. As a trained Career Development Practitioner, I find it easy to support others in realising their potential and self-worth. Unfortunately, when identifying strategies for my own progression in life and career, I am my worst critic and over think everything. I see every failing as a setback, doubting my worth initially as a person which then snowballs into being over critical about my contribution to my family, society and as a human being! On the outside everyone always thinks I am so sure of myself, but inside is filled with self-doubt.

Concepts of self-protection and self-nurturing in this chapter have caused me to reflect on how these negative feelings start. My inability to say no or set boundaries can then lead to burnout, feelings of not being good enough and a failure. I am already beginning to realise that asking for help is not a weakness and it's not always all on me. The phrase 'living creatively with my demons' in this chapter is powerful in assuring me that I can have failings, but I should not live by them and be so hard on myself."

Shayla Bletsoe, Career Development Practitioner & PhD student.

You don't have to do it!

When I was young, I was told I was responsible, polite, hard working. I was praised for helping others, told I was good with people. What made me happy was being tucked away in the art room, working with clay – the smell and texture, the pleasure in being so focused that I escaped from the sense of being a good girl. I was at peace. I was told I was good but didn't receive the same feeling of being valued, of mattering. I left art behind and explored all the helping/enabling professions.

Over 30 years later, here I am as a career coach, liking and believing in what I do, and being told I am good at it. But I am wondering if I am fully being my genuine self (equilibrium between my feelings, thoughts and actions)? The parts of my job that I enjoy the most are being on my own and designing presentations and writing materials. I enjoy my human interaction and indeed, that's where I get most of my ideas and inspiration, but if I have too much then I start to experience burn-out. So expanding the elements of your work where you are most at peace with yourself, can increase career happiness.

The trail of praise

How many people have followed the trail of other people's praise and encouragement, leaving behind more nourishing activities? Just because you are good at something, it doesn't mean that you need to dedicate yourself to it. You may have a "killer skill" that people value but end up being trapped by it.

When people say "it's not too late" they are often thinking of retraining, that may not feel feasible, financially and practically. So how can you change your career by stealth? You could tweak what you do, dabble in other areas, create a side-hustle with the possibility that it may lead to something. If what we're saying rings a bell, then this chapter is for you.

When you were young, what did other people praise you for? What encouragement did you receive?

↪

Describe

Maybe you didn't have encouragement - so what were you discouraged from doing that you did or could have enjoyed?

↪

Were the discouragers benefitting in any way – for example, were they threatened or anxious about what you enjoyed? Were they helped or reassured by the activities or qualities they praised?

An example of this would be "you'd be great working with children" as a thank you for helping them with babysitting. Their praise may be well intentioned but reflect their gratitude for your help, rather than a recognition of your potential.

↪

In your life, what activities, experiences and places,
- helped you to feel happy, calm, excited?
- led to a flow state (being in the present, focused and absorbed – time flowing by)?

Describe   **Draw**   **Cut and paste**

"Ah but ..."

If you are thinking that you are 'not good enough' at this activity or interest ...

a) what evidence have you got to support this belief?

b) remember how many years of experience, study, encouragement from others that it took to get you skilled in other areas. Add the word "yet" to the end of the statement – "I am not skilled enough, yet".

Changing career by stealth

People often think a career change requires significant retraining and starting at the bottom rung. Sometimes it does but you can always "be more crab" – moving sideways instead of up and down a ladder.

Consider your current role and, if you are employed, the company you work for:
- are there aspects of your job which reflect your interest that can be expanded?
- can you ask for opportunities to develop that interest?
- how about developing a side-hustle i.e. dabble with what interests you, attend a weekend workshop, volunteer until you feel skilled and confident enough to charge for your services. Then consider reducing your hours in your current role to pursue this interest.

Visualise

Describe

Shayla's reflections upon this chapter:

"I have been praised all my life for being helpful, caring, loving and always putting others first. In addition, having been 'good' at everything at school, it was expected that I would pursue an academic career, putting my intelligence to good use at university. The heavy weight of expectation from both aspects led me to pursue areas that others praised me for instead of being true to my 'genuine self'.

Now, at 36, I have seen that no matter how caring, helpful or intelligent I have been, I have still felt undervalued, under-appreciated and taken for granted, throughout my whole life. After reflecting on this chapter I can see how I am beginning to change my attitude towards my life and career. I am becoming more in tune with my 'genuine self' and incorporating my love of writing and performing into everyday life whether it be through paid work or just enjoyment. I am more mindful of what I want and need to be happy and find balance. This chapter reinforces my belief that I am on the right track towards building my 'own' success."

Shayla Bletsoe, Career Development Practitioner & PhD student.

Action and inaction (to go or to stop)

Can you think of times when you wanted to take action but didn't - maybe it was a career move and you didn't seize the opportunity? The healthy response is to work out why you didn't and to learn from the experience. A less healthy response is to be overly self-critical about it.

There's interesting research (see below) that explains why people don't take action, even when they want to. The same research also suggests that being hard on yourself doesn't help – in fact it increases your chances of staying stuck. So, let's look at the reasons why people don't take action and what they can do about it.

First of all, there may be external barriers and pressures, for example, finances, geography, caring responsibilities. Then there are the internal cognitive and psychological reasons why people don't take action or prematurely give up on their dreams.

The theory of career inaction (Verbruggen and De Vos 2020) identifies three phases of inaction:

1. the awareness phase in which we become aware of a desire to make a change,
2. the inaction phase, during which we fail to act, or act sufficiently,
3. the recall phase, in which we look back and feel regret for not having taken action. This phase is characterised by thoughts such as "if only I had ...", "I could have been ...", which lead to feelings of regret and self-blame.

Being hard on yourself actually increases the likelihood that you won't take action in the future. Understanding and having a bit of self-compassion is therefore a better response than "beating yourself up about it".

According to Verbruggen and De Vos, there are a number of reasons behind inaction, including:

- difficulties in making decisions ("*I'm hopeless at making decisions*"),
- anxiety about uncertain outcomes and potential losses ("*what if it doesn't work out?*"),
- pay offs for staying, winning over potential long-term gains (wages, conditions, security, good colleagues),
- cognitive overload/stress ("*it's all a bit too much*"),
- social norms ("*it's better to stick with what you know*"),
- fear of letting people down ("*we can't do without you; we don't want you to go*").

Have any of these reasons stopped you from making changes in the past that you now regret not making?

Reflect on these and capture your thoughts below:

Visualise

Describe

→

Are any stopping you now?

→

A way of testing to see if you really want to achieve your goals, is to visualise the future (in 1 year, 5 years or 10 years) and how you will feel if you haven't taken action.

- Imagine the worst-case scenario if you don't take action.

- Imagine the best-case scenario if you do take action.

Now scale your motivation to achieve this goal. What score will you give it at this moment? Mark your level of motivation on the line below:

0 - not bothered! ◄─────────────► 10 - I really want to!

Road people or river people?

Nightingale (1993) identified two groups of people to whom you can belong (you can belong to both groups):
- the river - happy splashing about and content where you are,
- the road - goal-orientated, deciding what you want, keeping your eyes on the goal and working until you reach it.

If you are around a 5 or below, then this might indicate that you are feeling ambivalent about making the change at this point in your life. Maybe you are the kind of person who likes to live in the moment, splashing about in the river and responding when your needs or the currents shift. At the moment you might be quite happy where you are and you don't feel pressed to set a goal or there might be a little bit of discomfort and you are ok with sticking with it until the need increases.

If you are not happy where you are and are still ambivalent about taking action, *"The fear / desire see-saw"* chapter may help to throw some light on what is causing the ambivalence.

Sustained motivation

If at this moment you feel highly motivated to achieve your goal, there are a number of ways that you can sustain this level of motivation and increase the likelihood of taking action:

- <u>Keep the worst-case and best-case scenario in mind</u> – write it down and recall what you imagined at regular intervals.
- <u>Make the future more concrete by crystallization</u> - gaining information, visioning/ inhabiting, reality testing via talking to people, shadowing etc (see chapters *"Distil your intent"* and *"I hope it rises"*).
- <u>Reduce the scale of change</u> - breaking down the process of change into smaller steps with short-term gains.
- <u>Reduce the timescale for action</u> - pressure can be motivational as there is less scope for procrastination. Inaction is in general less likely when the window of opportunity is shorter.
- <u>Find a career coach or mentor</u> – someone who can support and encourage you through the transition.

And remember, be kind to yourself – reframe self-critical thinking to "I haven't done it <u>yet</u>", "I learnt from the experience", "Each time I get a little closer".

Where do I start?

What if you are motivated and curious, but don't know what action to take? Read over these 3 approaches. If you find one of these approaches isn't for you, then try another!

The customary approach

This suggests that you start by clarifying your interests, values, skills and needs (the activities in this book will help). Doing this provides a blueprint to guide your research and quest to find opportunities that match your criteria. This is sometimes easier said than done because there are so many job titles out there and things keep changing. To aid this process, career websites tend to cluster jobs into industries, fields or "families" of related jobs so that you can start by identifying a cluster or job family that best reflects your blueprint.

Of course there is the question of which websites to trust? It's useful to look at who funds or runs the site and whether they have an agenda in how the information is presented. Many governments have impartial career information sites and can therefore be a trustworthy place to start. They may even provide job matching quizzes to kick start your exploration but please remember that such quizzes are meant to be food for thought rather than providing a perfect match.

Take a note of websites you have found or would like to use:

Describe

The purpose driven approach

If you want a job where you "make a difference" then this approach may be for you.

> In 2015 the United Nations identified 17 sustainable development goals to achieve by 2030. You should be able to easily find these by an internet search.
>
> - Reflect on areas that interest/are important to you.
>
> - Search for organisations that are involved in that area.
>
> - Use social media to follow those companies and find out more about their current projects.
>
> - Use professional social media sites such as LinkedIn to read the profiles of people who work for those companies and note your reactions to their job roles – would this be of interest to you? If so, connect with them and use an informational interview approach to find out more.

The curious approach

This entails a curious approach to scanning job sites, seeing what opportunities are in your locality and looking beyond familiar job titles – include those that may not initially interest you to check out your preconceptions. You never know what you may find! If remote or hybrid working is of interest to you, then search for opportunities based on this criteria. Curiosity will motivate you to check out jobs you may never have heard of before.

<u>Be nosey!</u>

Get into the habit of asking people about their work:
- what it entails,
- how they got into it,
- the good, bad and ugly bits (although remember that it's their perspective so not exactly objective!).

What question(s) would you like to ask? *Describe*

Let the opportunities come to you!

Recruiters use professional social media sites such as LinkedIn to find potential candidates, scanning for key words and skills in people's profiles. You therefore need to make sure that your profile is "future focused" using language that reflects where you want to go rather than what you're trying to leave behind.

There is a lot of free, on-line advice on how to do this. Also check that your settings allow alerts for opportunities. A useful approach is to look at the profiles of people who are in jobs that interest you and who are active on LinkedIn.

Capture what you could include in your profile. *Describe*

Suck it and see!

If time is critical and you need to earn some money, the best way to know if something will work or would be suitable is to give it a try.

Taking any action is better than doing nothing and getting stressed about it. Remember that you never know where an opportunity may lead.

What action will you take?
Describe

Becky's reflections upon this chapter:

This was a very thought-provoking chapter that helped me to reflect more deeply around why I sometimes fail to take action. I have often assumed that my own inaction stems from a fear-based belief that is out of my awareness. The chapter gave me a wider appreciation of the plethora of reasons why people may fail to take action. This allowed me to develop clearer insights around my own inaction and that my own inaction stems from a number of factors. This was new learning for me! This has deepened my awareness around the work I can now engage in that helps move me forward.

I also liked the contribution the chapter made to the concept of sustained motivation. I found the accompanying reframing techniques a helpful guide, to help me think and reflect more robustly. I'm often guilty of falling into black and white thinking and getting stuck in thinking loops. I will be using techniques like the future facing crystallisation technique to help in my own thinking and with the people I support.

Becky Marshall, Career Development Practitioner

Can you ... spot the difference?

How many differences can you spot?

You'll find the answer at the end of the chapter.

There is some debate around how many images (frames per second) that our eyes can see - on average the range is between 30 to 60 frames per second, which equates to around 240 million different images across an average person's lifespan. Each eye has a slightly different angled perspective which registers a slightly different image on the retina at the back of your eye. Your brain processes the two images within a fraction of a second, creating a 3-dimensional image.

Our self-image is equally complex and created. Your self-image draws on both your conscious and subconscious thoughts and beliefs, to create an internalised image or picture of yourself. Your self-image influences your actions, which in turn impacts on the decisions you make throughout your life and career.

The 3 dimensions of self-image:

1) How you perceive yourself.
2) What you believe other people's perceptions are about you.
3) Your ideal self, the way you would like to be.

On the next page capture your thoughts:

Describe   Draw   Cut and paste

How you see yourself.

What you believe other people's perceptions are about you.

Your ideal self, the way you would like to be.

Your interpretation of the 3 dimensions can influence how you feel (positive ⇌ negative). You are more likely to accomplish tasks when you are feeling positive about yourself than when you are feeling negative.

Human beings are complex - we are constantly constructing, de-constructing and re-constructing our self-image as we encounter new experiences and making sense of the world around us. We do not construct the view of ourselves in a vacuum - society is structured in a way that is not fully inclusive and therefore marginalisation can impact our self-image.

The UK Equality Act 2010; is a law which protects you from discrimination or unfair treatment on the basis of 9 protected characteristics:

- Age
- Disability
- Gender Reassignment
- Marriage and Civil Partnership
- Pregnancy and Maternity
- Race
- Religion or Belief
- Sex
- Sexual Orientation

Example: Jac, aged 21, wants to apply for a job within an organisation, but does not see anyone who they feel is <u>similar to them</u> on the company website or when visiting the company.

List the equality characteristics that Jac might be noticing when they are considering themselves to be different from other people in the organisation:

Describe

↳

Jac may have noticed a difference in any number of the 9 characteristics.

For reflection

Similarities or differences can relate to one protected characteristic but also range across multiple characteristics. The term "intersectionality" is often used to describe how a number of characteristics can intersect or overlap and create a unique experience for an individual. We are all different from each other. However, some people will experience a greater degree of difference.

Wobbly mirrors "do I fit?"

Our self-image can be influenced by whether we feel we fit – whether we see ourselves reflected back at us, telling us that we belong.

In a fairground, the Hall of Mirrors provides entertainment by distorting our reflection into peculiar shapes. What if your past experiences have led you to identify with the wobbly image rather than the true you?

Taking a step back to ask: is this really me? Is this perception of myself accurate? Have I allowed opportunities to pass by because I thought I wasn't the right person? What if I was?

→

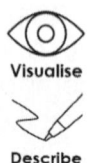

Imagine you have not spotted someone similar to you in a work environment, what might you say to yourself?

→

Your image and your career

Images within the media (including TV programmes and advertisements) have been gradually changing to reflect our society more accurately. Our self-confidence and wellbeing can stem from what we see and hear on a daily basis and therefore it is extremely important that the media continuously strives to uphold inclusivity.

In the mirror on the next page capture images that represent your SELF.

As you are doing this, double check that your assumptions (your wobbly mirror self), are not creating a distortion. Leave them out so that your image is clear.

Your mirror image:

Answer: 😀

Luisa's reflections upon this chapter:

"This chapter did make me reflect that for a long time I didn't perceive being an author as something I'd ever be able to achieve. I had an assumption that someone like me - girl who grew up in a council house, went to university on a full grant (and never earned enough to pay back the loans), never worked in anything similar to publishing or journalism etc - could never do it. I also didn't believe I was talented or clever enough.

Now I've proved it can be done, and networking has showed me that authors have lots of different backgrounds - and that many of them, like me, can't afford to write full-time. Even now I've proved my original idea wrong, I still have to fight against imposter syndrome and keep my self-talk as positive as possible to avoid becoming too discouraged - not always easy."

Luisa Andreou-Jones, Career Development Practitioner & Hybrid Author

Possibilities & Decisions

Chapter Titles: read the short statements and see which chapter(s) you are drawn to and sailplane from there.

I hope it rises

Life is rarely predictable, and Hope is an ingredient which can expand our thinking and helps us to imagine possibilities.

The pick 'n' mix isle

Curiosity around what influences your choices, can grow your confidence and help when planning the next step in your career.

I like strawberries, do you?

Regardless of the tone of voice used to ask this question, it still influences the listeners response.

Peeling the onion

The analogy of peeling back the layers of an onion has often been used to describe the exploration of your career story.

I Hope It rises

'I hope it rises' is something I have heard family members say in the process of baking a cake. Even though a recipe has been followed or knowledge applied (gained from many years of baking), there is still an element of hope. Hope, that the unseen factors behave as predicted (the leavening agent produces carbon dioxide bubbles, these are then trapped and expand during baking).

<u>HOPE</u> - the absence of answers OR a journey towards probabilities?

Life is rarely predictable, and "Hope" is an ingredient which can expand our thinking and helps us to imagine possibilities. Hope could be described as the absence of answers. But would this view motivate anyone to take action and move forward? Hope might be best described as a journey towards probabilities.

How would you describe hope? Write down some thoughts ...

Describe

Is hope a feeling, thought or a belief?

Sometimes we squash hope by moving too quickly to the stage of "yes, but..", focusing on the barriers and reasons why something may not work. The testing out ideas and the probabilities of what may work, usually comes later.

The metaphor of baking a cake can be used to explore the journey from possibilities to probabilities:

Step One
- *Decide what is needed – do you want something different or to use the same recipe that you have used before?*

Reflect on whether you are happy and content with how your career is unfolding, or do you see the potential for something new? Are you excited by the possibility of a different career?

Step Two
- *Explore possibilities – find new recipes, ask someone for ideas, go beyond what is familiar or revisit old recipes by adding new ingredients.*

Notice what is important to you within your career, but also what makes you anxious because it is unfamiliar. It could be that limiting thoughts are preventing the flow of possibilities. It may be helpful to discuss/gauge ideas with someone you know or a career development practitioner.

Step Three
- *Go for it – choose your recipe, buy your ingredients, get mixing.*

You now have a sense of direction. Your ingredients can include your existing skills (you already have them in the cupboard). But you also may need some new skills, qualifications, experience to put into the mix. It might take some time but holding onto the excitement of your initial vision can sustain your motivation.

Step Four
- *Tasting the mix – taking a spoon and checking the flavour (Probability).*

Often you need to get 'up close' to a potential career to help you move from possibility to probability. Maybe through work experience, shadowing, the support of a mentor, visiting an employer, applying for a job (even though you haven't fully decided if it is what you want). This testing stage will help you work out if you need to adapt your vision.

Step Five
- *Into the oven – watching your bake rise (Hoping).*

Starting to see your plans come to fruition – new connections with employers, some job interviews, expanding your network, positive references and recommendations.

Step Six

- *Patiently waiting – you may not see the cake rising anymore, but it is still cooking inside. The challenge is not to open the door too quickly (Sustain Hope).*

It can take time for your plans to come to fruition and it can be tempting to assume that it's not working and to give up. At this point getting back in touch your initial vision can help sustain hope. Encouragement from someone can help any waning beliefs.

Step Seven

- *Take it out of the oven – don't overbake.*

This is often some level of uncertainty when you get a job offer or new opportunity. If we procrastinate too long, waiting until we are sure that 'it is right', then we could miss the moment.

Step Eight

- *Enjoy and appreciate – share your success.*

Celebrate this success with friends and family.

Remember no career is perfect, so you can choose to refine your career recipe in the future.

Hopeful reflections

Sometimes it can be difficult to sustain Hope.

Think of a time in the past when you have kept going despite not knowing whether something is going to work out.

What helped you to keep going?
Describe

What advice would you give someone who was struggling to sustain Hope?

Jennifer's reflection upon this chapter:

"LOVED this chapter. Hope is so important yet difficult to define. Relating the steps of baking a cake really connected with me. Step six reminded me how I felt when I was at university doing my post-graduate diploma. My family really had to step in and encourage me to keep me going because I lost it a few times. That relates to how you feel when you can't see your cake because it's in the oven. I especially can't see my cakes at the moment because my oven light is broken. This chapter put into words, how you can feel during a time of change.

In baking, when you are trying something new, if it doesn't work out, you still have your old recipes to fall back on. And, if the worst happens, you can get something at the shop. However, you can also fantasise that if it turns out well that you could eventually be ready to apply for a certain TV show and have your baking talent acknowledged with the elusive 'handshake'. Dream.

The baking analogy could be used to encourage someone I am supporting to look back on their experience, in a stage-by-stage way, and consider if anything could have been changed that might have led to a different outcome. *Did you forget an ingredient or was one of your ingredients out of date?* You could then move the discussion onto reflecting on what has been learned. *Was it a complete disaster or can we salvage some of the sponge and make a trifle?*"

Jennifer Convery, Career Development Practitioner

The pick 'n' mix isle

Woolworths used to be a shop which sold everything, including records, paint and pyjamas. It had a famous (or some parents might say infamous) pick 'n' mix isle - it was the first of its kind, a concept now found in many shops and cinemas. Woolworth's shelves had a huge choice of rainbow-coloured sweet treats, different sizes and textures. Some were even shaped to resemble 'real' food, for example, white chocolate fish portions.

The biggest challenge was trying to stay within your pocket money budget. The only way to keep your indulgence in check was to place your partly filled sweetie bag on the shiny, silver, scales and monitor the weight as you gradually added another and another treat.

Pick 'n' Mix is still a popular treat for children and adults alike. With a huge choice available, the factors that influenced each person is varied. Each pick with the tongs can be based on thoughts including:

> I like real strawberries and these look-like strawberries.
>
> My friend has picked 3 of these, they must be good.
>
> That colour is my favourite.
>
> I have tasted this before and I know I like it.
>
> This sweet smells good, so it should taste good too.
>
> Marshmallows are light, so I can get more for my money.

Add a thought of your own

Describe

It is understandable that the contents of each person's sweetie bag could be compared by its uniqueness, to that of their fingerprint.

Choosing your career

Your career is influenced by a wide range of factors and includes elements of logic and intuition as well as conscious and subconscious thought.

Career websites have a huge choice of careers. Some sites have over 12,000 careers listed and still state that their list is not exhaustive. The world of work is continually evolving, fed by social changes and emerging technologies. Children currently in primary school will have access to careers that do not exist today. In contrast, some careers are disappearing or changing rapidly, requiring individuals to face difficult decisions.

Making a decision can feel tough and so being curious about what influences your choices, can grow your confidence and help when planning the next step in your career.

Let's use the metaphor of the Pick 'n' Mix aisle, to consider what environmental factors were important to you at the point of leaving education and what fundamental things still influence your choice of career.

<u>Step one</u>:

Read the selection of words below. Pick from the words or come up with your own to capture what is important to you now. <u>Write the words into the sweet shapes on the next page</u>.

These words are just a starting point and to prompt your own thoughts:

Indoors / Outdoors	Fast / Slow
Talking / Listening	Large Company / Small Business
Noisy / Quiet	Lots of People / Few People
Facts / Possibilities	Routine Hours / Various Shifts
Caring / Construction	Continually Learning / Be an expert
Practical / Theoretical	Responsible / Carefree
Creative / Routine	Numbers / Words

Step two:

Prioritise which are the most important to you, by numbering the sweets from **1 through to 7**.

Our taste buds change every 7 years

Our taste buds are formed of a cluster of differentiated epithelial cells and neurons found in the tongue and palate. These cells are active in two ways: they are excited sensory receptors which communicate <u>and,</u> are at the same time being renewed around every 2 weeks.

It is no surprise that our taste changes. These changes within our taste receptors can relate to discovering new flavours, our health, or simply because we are getting older.

Similarly, what is important to us within our life and work is subject to change, because we are continually exposed to new experiences and need to balance a range of priorities.

Thinking back, are there things that used to be important but they have faded away. What were they?
Describe

Previously, you may have thought or said "I'm not creative", however since discovering creativity (verb) and developing this skill, you now feel creativity is important within your life and career. You no longer view creativity as a noun, something static that you are or are not.

Thinking about your needs, what are you priorities today? Capture what you are visualising.

Describe   Draw   Cut and paste

Reflection

Read over the things that are important to you (captured and prioritised in the sweets), including what is important to you today compared to the past.

Select the 3 things that are the most important to you today and expand your thoughts.

↪

Describe

Reflecting on your priorities how satisfied are you with the balance across your life and work?

Describe

Are there changes or actions needed? What steps could you take?

↪

Four of the people who have provided chapter reflections within the book have also provided three of the most important things in their current life and career:

Jen:
1) Purpose – living with intention.
2) Alignment – finding the right balance for me.
3) Courage – leading with curiosity instead of fear.

Erin:
1) Challenging myself – I love to learn new things.
2) Helping others – that keeps me motivated.
3) Keeping active – that's when I'm most creative.

Heather:
1) Financial independence – finding a career I love and pays well.
2) Helping others – validates my value and increases my self-worth.
3) Challenging thinking – the feeling of being alive, and a good tired.

Alex:
1) Helping others – whether it's formally teaching or informally supporting peers.
2) Challenging thinking – people's self-perceptions, the status quo in a place/team, and most importantly…my own beliefs and biases!!
3) Achieving results – however defined: hard, soft, personal, team – something that allows me to acknowledge and celebrate progress.

We might choose a job based on one set of priorities for example, money. However the reason why we seek a change is often due to an increased awareness as to priorities that are not being met for example, workplace culture or work/life balance. Therefore examining what is important to you, going beyond your immediate needs, can lead to greater satisfaction within your life and career.

I like strawberries, do you?

Regardless of the tone of voice used to ask this question, it still influences the listener's response. If this question was asked in a bullish manner, then some people who don't like strawberries might opt for a seemly polite response in an attempt to avoid potential disagreement - "they are not my *favourite* fruit".

As a child I enjoyed the Wimbledon tennis fortnight. It was a sign of summer and school holidays being only weeks away. Within a day or two of the tournament starting, many friends and neighbours dusted off their tennis rackets or actively went to buy a shiny new one. The patience of many end terrace households would be tested as children worked to improve their skills, by playing 'keepy uppies' against their outside walls. The influence of this sport was clear to see, but for most eager participants, their rackets were back in the cupboard or garage soon after the Wimbledon tournament finished.

With the expanding access to information and the growth of media sources, the extent to how we are influenced has also grown. Influence can be subtle, almost invisible, the message persuasive and the receiver unaware of its effect. Or it can be blatantly obvious when the receiver makes a conscious decision to accept or reject the message being conveyed.

Mass media can affect who we vote for, the food we eat, plus our personal beliefs. There is also the potential for false information to skew our opinions and attitudes. Companies and individuals rely on their ability to influence our opinion of their products and services. The loss of trust in a product or damage to a reputation, can have a huge impact on profits and the ability for a company to survive. Therefore, increasing or protecting image is important - many individuals and companies employ a media guru to critique and advise on how to enhance their influence.

2009 saw the inauguration of the 'Influencer Phenomenon', where hobbies grew into new, life-changing careers as social media influencers. Over the past decade Bloggers and YouTubers have evolved into industry leaders, fashioning huge platforms of followers, generating an income from views and their endorsement of products.

What and who are your influencers and influences?

From birth we are influenced by the environment and people around us - these carry into our career decisions. During adolescence and early adulthood we unify our collection of influencers, identifications, and role models, pruning and strengthening an alliance with elements that reflect our emerging identity and sense of self. *Unlike* role models, parents/carers are given to us and so we may or may not choose to include them.

Reflecting on who and what influences you, will help you to understand their impact on your current and future decision making. Influence comes in two forms:

Influencers (people, guides)
Influences (structures, experiences)

Mapping both Influencers and Influences will help you to see their potential to impact your choices. Thereafter you can decide whether to accept, prune the influence, or to actively widen your sphere by seeking other sources.

Who are your influencers?

Write down the names of whoever comes into your mind. They could be real or fictional, alive or dead, directly in your life or a media role model.

Describe   Draw

Draw a circle in the centre of a page.
Add 3 or 4 outer circles.
Draw yourself in the middle of the circle (can be as simple as a stick person) or write your name if you're not in the mood for drawing.

Take the first name in your list of people and ask yourself ... how important are they to me? Depending on their level of influence, decide in which circle to write their name. The closer to you, the stronger the influence. Continue the exercise for your other influencers.

Once you have finished, use the questions below to reflect the different roles each influencer has. A person could occupy a number of roles:

• Who is a mentor?	• Who is a doubter?
• Who is an advocate?	• Who is a protector?
• Who is a challenger?	• Who is an ally?
• Who is a saboteur?	• Who is a fairy godfather/mother?
• Who is an inspiration?	• Who is an encourager?
• Who is a distractor?	• Who is a logistician (resources)?
• Who is a connector?	• Who is a doorperson?
• Is there anyone who plays a role not listed above, what title would you give them?	

Influencers by design

Imagine you were able to design the ideal network of positive influencers. Who would you choose to be in your inner and outer circles?

Review your existing circles and ask yourself:
- Do I need different people around me?
- Do I have the right people in my inner circles?

Visualise

Draw a new set of circles and place your Influencers in positions for optimum support.

Alternatively ...
Use your original circles, highlight names and draw arrows to where you would like your Influencers to be positioned.

What are your influences (structures, experiences)

On a separate page capture the different environments that you have encountered.

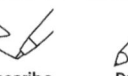
Describe   Draw

Cut and paste

They could be buildings or places relating to hobbies, work, social, personal, learning, holidays. For inspiration have a look at your past internet search history – what made you smile ☺

Pick one of your environments.
Imagine you are there, what feelings arise?
Use the space below to capture your thoughts or draw emojis. Repeat this activity for a few of the environments.

Describe   Draw

→

What does this tell you about the environments where you feel more positive than negative?
Did any patterns or themes emerge?

→

Influences by design

Imagine you were able to design the ideal positive environment.

On a separate piece of paper use these questions as prompts to help you create your ideal environment:

- What would it look like?
- What sounds can you hear?
- What can you smell?
- Where would it be?
- What would you be doing?
- What would you be feeling?
- Would anyone else be there?

Describe   Draw   Cut and paste

How can you use the picture of this place?
- Does picturing it help manage your stress?
- Does it ground you?
- Does it tell you anything about what you need in life?
- Does it restore your sense of self?

<u>Using this activity with others</u> ...

You can use sticky notes to write down the names or modelling clay, building blocks to create figures of people.

        Describe Model

If you are a school teacher then the activity could be linked to a topic, for example, English Literature and Social Subjects such as History or Politics.

Elaine's reflections upon this chapter:

"Thinking about this chapter, I was struck as to how this resonated with some of the personal issues I have been grappling with in terms of my own identity and self-care. I love stand-up comedy, and one of my favourite comedians is Stewart Lee. He posed the question, 'can you have a context-free word?' and when I think about people, I wonder if any individual really exists in an influence-free bubble.

When making decisions or setting a course of action, how many of us do so without consideration of others? Recently I have been trying to uphold healthy boundaries for myself. With a constant stream of commitments to work, family, and friends, I frequently find myself making decisions based on what others want or need from me. Amid this, I've started to ask myself how I can make room for me in my own life. How do we gain a healthy balance of trying to be caring and considerate human beings, while also upholding boundaries for ourselves? I'm going to endeavour to make more space for me and my needs, but it's tough. Especially when my behaviours and decisions in life are rarely influence-free.

Just as no word can really have true meaning without context, I don't think any individual can really exist without being influenced by the people, structures, and experiences that encompass them."

Elaine Whates, Career Development Practitioner

Peeling the Onion

The analogy of peeling back the layers of an onion has often been used to describe the exploration of your career story. The skin of the onion represents the surface – what you tell people if you are short of time. Underneath the skin is the full story of your experiences - what you have learnt about yourself and the world, the life skills you have acquired, your comfort zone and your potential (the abilities, qualities, values and interests that are yet to emerge).

You may already be aware of the inner layers and know what is helping and hindering you.

If you seek support from a Career Development Practitioner, then they will help you to peel back the layers, discover new insights, and gain clarity as to resources are already in place and what could be strengthened. Whilst we can use this book to reflect, other people may be able to reflect back what we are missing or not seeing.

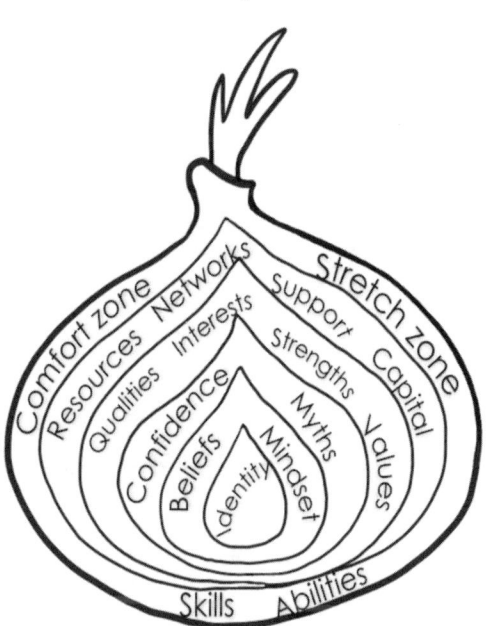

Decisions behind the decisions

Sometimes we are struggling to make a decision because we are only looking at the surface and fail to spot that there is another decision lying behind that is the crux of the issue. If that decision is made then the surface decisions will suddenly fall away.

Your layers ...

Write down a decision you are facing:

Write down any decisions lying behind this decision that may need to be made first:

<u>Tears are normal</u>

Peeling onions usually make people cry. Likewise, tears can be part of the decision-making process but they can be good tears, for example:

- relief at being listened to and understood if you are talking this through with someone,

- getting in touch with what you need to let go of, grieving for what you are choosing to leave behind.

References: *This chapter is adapted from Hambly, L. and Bomford, C. (2019:139) Creative Career Coaching, Theory into Practice.*

Deirdre's reflections upon this chapter:

""I love the analogy of peeling the onion back to discover one's inner self. I remember when I was a young mother with two young children, having moved from Bristol to a quiet village in Derbyshire with my husband for his new job. I felt displaced from the world of work.

I had trained earlier as a professional careers adviser, but I couldn't find the right solution to building my confidence and finding a way back into paid employment. I made an appointment to meet a professionally trained careers adviser, 'Rosie'. Step by step, she reminded me to peel back the hidden layers.

She reminded me of:

(i) the importance of taking time for reflection,
(ii) writing down the things that were important to me, and
(iii) not rushing into things.

The only person who was putting me under pressure was myself!"

Associate Professor Deirdre Hughes OBE and
Co-founder of CareerChat UK Ltd

Influences and Influencers

Chapter Titles: read the short statements and see which chapter(s) you are drawn to and sailplane from there.

Walls: boundaries, safety or confinement?

Walls are often used as metaphors to convey a range of experiences & emotions, most commonly to express something getting in the way.

Who is driving your bus?

The people we regularly engage with or have previously engaged with influence our view of the world and ourselves.

A high functioning crew

When we face life-career choices we may find we know what to do, or we can feel torn, conflicted, not knowing which way to turn.

A basket of crabs or a pod of dolphins

Did you know that a basket of live crabs doesn't need a lid on it and that dolphin pods collaborate to protect and help each other?

Walls: boundaries, safety or confinement?

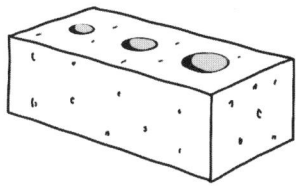

We are surrounded by physical walls. They provide structured spaces for life and work, when interacting with others or having time alone. In the 19th century many stately homes built walled gardens to regulate the environment to produce high quality flowers, fruit, vegetables (and keep unwanted poachers out). Also around this time was the founding of the first state prison, where walls were used to separate individuals from the wider population. Throughout the generations, the appearance of walled structures has evolved to reflect societal evolution and trends. Nonetheless, the primary function of a wall remains constant - a structure to keep someone or something, within or out of a designated space.

Walls are often used as metaphors to convey a range of experiences and emotions, most commonly to express something getting in the way (a barrier).

"It's like hitting my head against a brick wall!"

When imagining this action, you may see something painful and pointless, yet someone else could envisage a different wall and interpretation. One individual asked to picture a wall, described a low, mossy covered, dry stone wall, easy to climb over using a stile. Overall their view was a pleasant experience with the wall representing a transition point (marker) within their life journey.

Metaphoric walls can be built by us or constructed from circumstances that we encounter. These walls can appear as difficult to pass as real physical structures. Their size, width, depth, texture, colour can be as unique as you.

At this moment in time, do you feel that you have something getting in the way of your life or work? Is something stopping you from moving forward? This activity can help your explore barriers and consider different perspectives.

You can approach the following activity in 3 ways:

1) start with the metaphor and reflect on what it means afterwards,
2) hold a life experience in mind,
3) reflect on a wall you have dreamed about (as you feel ready to explore its meaning).

Your view of the wall

This activity will guide you through creating a distant and close up view of a wall. You can do this by visualising a picture in your mind or, you might prefer to describe, draw or cut/paste on a separate page.

Take one question at a time and gradually create a view of the wall. Some questions contain examples to help prompt your thinking.

Describe your view of the wall:

- How tall is the wall?
- How wide is the wall?

- Where is your wall?
  - is it part of anything?
  - how close are you to it?

- What is the wall made from?
  - bricks and mortar
  - wood panelling
  - dry stone
  - roughcasting
  - tiling
  - plaster
  - painted render

- Are they any designs, pictures, graffiti on the wall?
  - mosaics
  - drawings
  - colours

- How long has the wall been there?

- Who does the wall belong to?

Visualise

Describe

Draw

Cut and paste

Let's explore the wall in more detail?

- ➢ What does the wall feel like to the touch?
  - ○ hot / cold
  - ○ rough / smooth
  - ○ straight / angled
  - ○ dry / wet / damp

- ➢ Can you see over, through or around the wall?

- ➢ How will you access the view on the other side of the wall, what is it?
  - ○ a loose brick
  - ○ a crack
  - ○ a door
  - ○ a window
  - ○ a foothold

- ➢ Describe what you see.

- ➢ How familiar is this view?

- ➢ How do you feel about this view?

<u>Take a few steps back from the wall:</u>

Review your answers to the questions above and consider whether there are any thoughts, feelings or perspectives that you have not previously noticed.

Describe

When a wall is within our view, the options are to:

1) accept its presence in its entirety,
2) accept its presence but make some alterations,
3) explore how to move past, through or over the wall,
4) knock it down.

What would you like to do to your wall?

Describe

Remove the metaphor and bring into focus the barrier within your life represented by the wall.

Reflection:
- On a scale of 1-10, (1 is not at all motivated, and 10 is totally motivated) how motivated are you to tackle the wall?

- On a scale of 1-10, (1 is completely unable, and 10 completely able) how able are you to move past the wall?

It is normal that we can face many different practical or emotional elements that confine us and prevent us moving forward, for example, *money, anxiety, cognitive overload, expectations of other people, fear of failure.*

Identifying the first step (even a small step), can lead to successfully addressing your wall.

Review or write down answers to the questions below:

Describe

- What would help you:
  - to accept its presence in its entirety?
  - to accept its presence but make some alterations?
  - to explore how to move past, through or over the wall?
  - to knock it down?

- a reason / ambition ... why?

- a person/people ... who?

- a tool or resource ... which?

- a timescale ... when?

- an opportunity ... where?

After working through this activity, if you still feel that you are struggling with the wall because there are elements that are outside of your control, then joining with other people who feel the same way can generate hope and strength for collective action.

Another point in time:

If you try this activity on another day, your wall may be different and lead to fresh insights.

Beth's reflections upon this chapter:

"I'm someone who usually shies away from using this type of reflective activity with individuals I support, but it worked so well on me, I need to rethink that attitude. This activity was like a revelation for me. It helped me to view one of my barriers from a more objective perspective and that distance was surprisingly emotive. In describing it as a wall, it gave me a clarity I've not seen before. It brought to mind that lovely saying by Dr Wayne Dwyer 'when you change the way you look at things, the things you look at change.'

I used the boundaries metaphor for a life circumstance of mine, it's not new and I've made slow progress using various talking techniques. I followed the instructions and drew it as a wall. Seeing it's size in a drawing next to me was upsetting. How had I let it get so big...almost as big as me...how did I not notice it's size before? No wonder it feels all encompassing. But through drawing it as a wall I could see it from a fresh perspective. It's a big complex wall comprising of colourful gems that energise me and other ugly stones that make me sad and overwhelmed.

When I described it, I realised it was made up of natural and organic materials, and a penny dropped. Maybe it's understandable that it grew so big, because natural and organic matter can grow slowly and go unnoticed. The activity helped me realise I want to break this wall down but not get rid of it; I want to keep the good bits & therein lies my actions. My work is to recognise the good stones, the gems that turn up my brightness and think about ways to keep them, whilst discarding the unhelpful stones."

Beth Urquhart, Career Development Practitioner

Who is driving your bus?

🎵 'She'll be coming round the mountain when she comes' 🎵

You may have heard or sung this tune. It originated in the USA, back in the 1940's. For decades in Scotland, this melody has been coupled with different words and verses, often sung by children going on a school trip by bus.

🎵 'Ye canny shove yer grannie aff a bus.

Ye canny shove yer grannie aff a bus.

Ye canny shove yer grannie, cause she's yer mammie's mammie

Ye canny shove yer grannie aff a bus.' 🎵

As a young child, I remember thinking, "why would you even want to shove your grannie off of a bus?" It was a puzzlement.

Grannies are often portrayed as welcoming, cheery people who are interested in everything you have been doing, even the smallest thing, and they burst with pride celebrating every achievement large or small. However other grannies are portrayed as grumpy, critical, mood hoovers who suck up all positivity, only to replace it with their own cynical view of the world.

Imagine you are on a bus journey accompanied by one of those critical grannie figures. Whatever interesting topic or plan you mention, they dampen your enthusiasm and positivity, saying *'you don't want to do that'* or *'that will never work'* or *'you're not smart enough'*. Stopping the bus and letting them off to visit their favourite tea shop, sounds like a good move. It would allow you to get on with the journey undisturbed, and in a more positive frame of mind.

The driver's seat

The people we regularly engage with or have previously engaged with, can influence our view of the world and ourselves. Whether through direct interactions or vicarious experiences (observing others, including media and personalities) their influence can be unnoticed and underestimated.

Even when separated from the person, their words and influence may continue to impact your thoughts, feelings and decisions.

Using the image of the inside of a bus (<u>on the next page</u>):

- Write your name in the driver's seat of the bus.

- Write on the seats of the bus, the names of people (past or present) who influence you.
Describe

  You may hear their words, opinions or voice in your head when in certain situations.

  <u>A tip:</u> use a pencil so you can move people around the bus.

- Notice who is sitting close to the driver's seat and who is sitting nearer the back.
Visualise

Reflect on whether any of these characters are "backseat drivers", instructing and directing you.
Visualise

They may even try to take hold of the steering wheel.
Describe

What might they be saying to you?

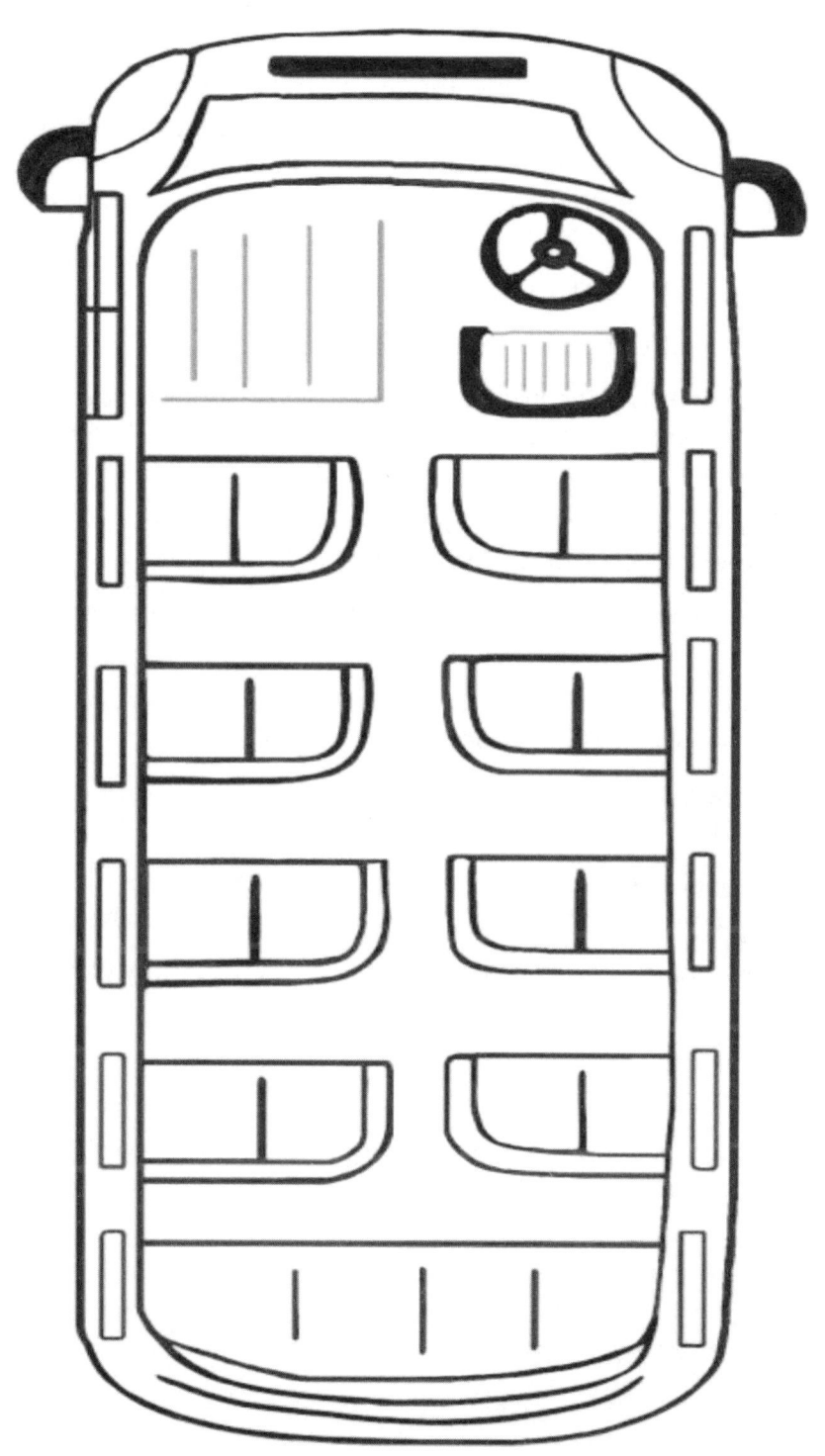

Saboteurs

This image of a critical grannie represents the kinds of people in our lives who feed our inner saboteurs. These saboteurs were initially developed when we were young to protect us in some way. The problem is they are still hanging around and undermining our self-worth and progress.

Chamine (2012) identified 10 saboteurs:

Judge - over critical of yourself and others.

Victim - which has been hurt in the past but continues to see the world through that lens, feeling helpless, sad and frustrated. Would like others to rescue them.

Pleaser - seeks approval and worth by helping and being nice to others. Needs to be liked to feel good.

Restless - avoids discomfort by moving on, seeking excitement and the new.

Hyper-vigilant - continuously worries about what may go wrong, spotting potential risks and danger.

Hyper-achiever - self-worth is linked to working hard and achieving success. Often highly driven and a workaholic.

Hyper-rational - self-worth is linked to knowledge, logic and understanding. Feelings are controlled or understood in this way.

Controller - being in control of the situation keeps anxiety and uncertainty at bay.

Stickler - perfectionist, organised and methodical. Setting high standards and following processes in a rather inflexible way.

Avoider - avoids uncomfortable feelings and situations by sticking to the comfort zone, procrastinating and focusing on the pleasant and positive.

If you can spot that you have any of these, then you're not alone – people don't write books on a subject where there isn't an audience waiting to say, "that's me!"

Builders

Builders are like the positive grannie. These people are interested in you, celebrate your achievements and when you are struggling, encourage and help you to build a growth mindset. Builders can help you construct and maintain healthy, positive self-efficacy behaviours:

Self-compassion – rather than judging yourself, you accept that any saboteurs are for a reason. They were developed when young to protect you in some way, to earn you the love and acceptance of others. They wouldn't be there if they hadn't worked in the past.

Self-development (laying new stones) - in the chapter "*A high functioning crew*" we consider how you can build stronger self-worth by developing sides of yourself that have been squashed or supressed, for example the confident, assertive, adventurous you.

Self-nurturing - paying attention to what nourishes you and building more of it into your life, even when pushed for time. For example, your environment, nature, senses, rituals, massage, exercise, good food, sleep, meditation.

Self-protecting - commitment to setting boundaries, practicing saying "no" or "leave it with me, I'll think about it", to small and easier demands so that you're ready for the bigger challenges. Envision a shield around you that lets good things in but keeps out other people's negativity. Make a map of the people around you and notice who pulls you down and who makes you feel good – move the negative people further away on the map and choose to spend less of your time and energy with them (or protect yourself if you have no choice).

Self-forgiveness - think of things you are critical of yourself for having done or not done. Ask yourself what kind things you would say to someone else in the same situation. Phrasing forgiveness statements and imagine saying them to those people and then yourself.

Self-responsibility - compassion for oneself needs to be combined with taking responsibility as well. Blame seems to be one-sided – it's either your fault or mine. In contrast, taking responsibility acknowledges the part we may have played in what happened as well as their part. Therefore, we all take responsibility - no one person is to fully blame, and shame is avoided *(with exception of harm as a result of illegal activity)*.

Self-sharing - making a difference, sometimes with the smallest of actions or gifts. When you feel low and tired, it might be difficult to think of doing something for others. However doing so can top up your self-worth battery. We might tell young people that they are loved and valued, but to develop true self-worth adolescents need opportunities to experience success. As adults we are no different – we need to feel we make a difference.

Saboteur and builder fusion

People and our relationships with them are often complex. Sometimes a person may be both a saboteur and a builder - there may be aspects of them and their behaviour that build you up and other aspects that break you down.

Colour your passengers

(you will need highlighters or coloured pens/pencils).

Draw

- Return to the image of your bus.

- Pick a colour to represent a person who feeds your saboteurs.

- Use this colour to highlight or shade in the seats of people who undermine (you may choose to partly colour a seat to represent the volume of negative influence – see example below).

- Pick a colour to represent a person who builds you up.

- Highlight or colour in the seats of people who are builders (you may choose to partly colour a seat).

Example:

Brother

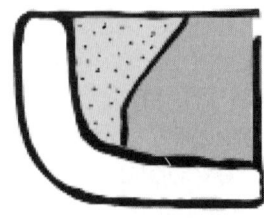

What's to happen with grannie?

You are now stopping at your service station or a rest stop. Turn around and look around your bus.

Are you happy with ...
- who is on your bus?
- where they are sitting?
- the influence they have over your ability to drive the bus?

Visualise

Is there anyone you want to move further away, to the back of the bus, where they have less influence?

Is there anyone you want to move forward near the front of the bus, where they can support, encourage and alert you to any saboteurs?

Is there anyone you would like off the bus completely? To leave behind for now or forever? It might be helpful to imagine them being in a setting that they would be happy in, for example, a café, nature reserve or shopping centre.

Are there people real or imaginary (friend, new partner, mentor, confidant) who you would like to bring onto the bus? What will these people contribute?

As you continue on your journey you might find that some of the people who you moved towards the back or left behind, can sneak back on or towards the front. So keep your eye on the rear-view mirror and enlist the support of your builders to alert you or block their presence.

Reflection

Are there any conversations you need to have with your builders to help you maintain control of your direction?

Is there any other action that you need to take to build a positive network of support?

Sometimes letting go can be a tricky process and you might find it helpful to talk it through with someone who can support you in a professional or informal way.

Laurence's reflections upon this chapter:

"Who is driving your bus" is really at the heart of managing your life and career. How often to you stop to notice who is influencing you and whether these connections are positively or negatively impacting your choices? The activities within this chapter can provide discernment that leads you to acknowledge the manner in which other people interact with your plans and ambitions."

Laurence Bayston, Career Development Practitioner & Area Manager

Beth's reflections upon this chapter

"This chapter encouraged me to get really curious about the influences in my life and the impact they have (even on my thoughts). What I want to do next in my life is not what I've done in the past and it helped me question if I'm paying too much attention to the people on my bus who, although they have my best interests at heart, their voices are around safety. I've been listening to someone who's hyper vigilant and someone who's a stickler and although I'm in the driving seat, I've had them sitting really close.

If I'm going to tackle my next decision differently, I might need builders who are courageous & supportive. The bus is a great visual for helping me recognise this, I was rubbing out names and moving them around. I do have builders in my life and maybe by moving them to the front of my bus I can listen to their voices and help change things in my reality too."

Beth Urquhart, Career Development Practitioner

A High Functioning Crew

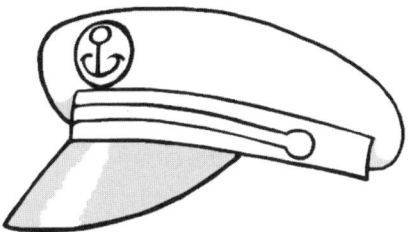

Where wind meets the ocean, fuelling a storm or filling sails to aid speedy passage; where horizons strain the eye or catch a glimpse of land, signalling the journey's end. No wonder the sea is often used as a metaphor for the career journey. This chapter considers the role of the crew – the team of people, each with a role to play, a team that can be mutinous or harmonious. In a high functioning crew, the value of each role will be recognised and brought to the fore to adapt and steer ships through different waters.

Your inner crew

We have many dimensions to our personality, many sides or parts that come out depending on who we are with, the context we find ourselves in and the challenges we face. Sometimes we are brave, other times afraid, sometimes confident, other times full of self-doubt, sometimes playful, other times serious. And so on. When we face life-career choices we may find that we just know what to do – the path is clear, there is no inner conflict. Then there are times when we feel torn, conflicted, not knowing which way to turn - we feel at war with ourselves, undermined by our own thoughts and feelings, our habits and anxieties.

Carl Jung believed that our "self" is made up of many parts, sides or aspects, which he called archetypes. Conflict arises when we are out of balance, for example, when a part is dominant, undermining or squashing another part. A classic example is the inner critic who can undermine our more confident or playful self. Our upbringing and life experience will have shaped what tends to be more dominant in us. Some parts may be so squashed that we have no sense that they are there. These squashed parts might be vital crew members that we need to bring out from below the decks and give voice to.

A good place to start is to reflect on:

- the voices or parts that come out in different contexts,

- those that are very familiar and dominant,

- those that were helpful in the past (keeping you safe) but are now holding you back,

- those you'd like to find and give shape and voice to.

The following are based on Jung's archetypes. Highlight any of these that ring true for you.

Playful child	Healer	Teacher	Victim	Guide	Wounded child
Hero / Heroine	Networker	Father	Mother	Rebel	Abandoned child
Warrior	Inner critic	Sceptic	Martyr	Mentor	Sceptic/ Questioner
Rescuer	Saboteur	Artist	Athlete	Pioneer	Storyteller
Servant	Addict	Builder	Mediator	Clown	Puppet
Friend	Performer	Messenger	Writer	Creative	Hedonist
King / Queen	Princess / Prince	Destroyer			

Rather than use Jung's archetypes, you can think about the sides of yourself that help/hinder and give them your own name.

Examples below, plus space for your names ...

Cool cat	Confident me	Risk-taker	Assertive	Sensible
Good	Workhorse	Observer	Party-animal	Introvert
Extravert	Dog with a bone	Perfectionist	Sloth	Anxious worrier

Once you know your inner crew, it's important to realise that you can't get rid of any – they are part of you and have been useful in the past. As captain, you can thank them for the role they have played and ask them to retire to their cabin or take a nap in the hold. Those that might be more useful can now take up more space and help to make the journey smoother, successful and enjoyable. The captain can choose the crew they want around them, ask for advice, listen to what they say and choose the best way forward.

Your captain

Your captain is your wise self – a strong crew manager, willing to listen, resolve conflict and develop each member's capabilities.

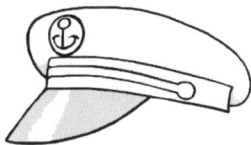

Imagine your captain as you would like them to be. The shape, sound, aura.
Imagine stepping into this image and feel what it is like to be that captain. Use emojis or describe how you feel:

 Visualise

 Describe   Draw

Your captain can view the whole crew and encourage the more reluctant and quieter voices to be heard.

Giving shape and voice to your reluctant crew

Some of your quieter sides may not find it easy to take up space. You may even struggle to believe that they exist. However, a captain's role includes supporting the development of their crew.

Turn your attention to a quality that you'd like to develop.
What name will you give it? For example: confident / assertive / risk-taker.   Insert the name you have chosen:

You are now going to be asked questions to build an image.
Choose from one or more of these methods:

 Describe    Draw   Cut and paste    Visualise   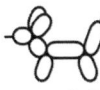 Model

What does it look like? It could be a person, animal, object or shape.
↪

Filling in the details. What is its colour, size, texture.
↪

What encouraging words will help it grow - what reassurance does it need to take up more space in your life?
↪

If your image is small and shadowy, make it grow by giving it colour and form.
↪

What is its voice like? If it is quiet and hesitant, encourage it to be stronger. How has the voice changed?
↪

What would it like to say about your current situation/dilemma?
↪

Does it need reassurance from the captain? How else could the captain reassure/convey that this crew member has an important contribution to make?
↪

Anchoring

A ship's anchor is used to steady the ship and prevent drift. If you are in the process of breaking old habits of thinking and being, then an anchor prevents drift and moors you to new thoughts and behaviour.

Find your anchor to create a psychological and emotional link to stimulate or remind you of your new state of mind, for example, an item of clothing or jewellery that you associate with this change. This anchor will provide stability whilst the change is embedding.

Alternatively, create an anchor, perhaps a stone of a certain colour and texture with writing the name or drawing an image on. You can keep this item on view or in your pocket.

STONES with words or pictures

Lorna carries a stone in her pencil case, with an apple core drawn on it, which represents 'exercising inner strength'. Each day reaching for a pen, reminds her that she has inner strength which can be drawn upon.

In some fields of personal development, this is called a transitional object – by giving something form then you are bringing this into being, supporting the inner process with an outer manifestation.

Alex's reflections upon this chapter:

"I've read this chapter three times now and haven't been sure what to write. Not because I've got nothing to say, but because metaphors like this engage me on such a visceral level, I'm never sure how much to disclose; so hopefully I've got the balance right!

Having changed career recently, I found the content of this chapter really helped me to decontextualise some aspects of the journey I've found most difficult.

In my last job, I felt I had such a good handle on my "inner crew" – giving all the good shifts to the members who'd served me best (coach, guide, enabler, challenger, defender, integrity), so much so that I truly believed I'd retired the ones who'd always rocked the boat and thrown me off-course (insecurity, self-consciousness, perfectionist, anxious worrier, approval-seeker, risk-averse).

It was this confidence in my inner crew that allowed me to take the plunge and change career completely, but as it turns out, my old crew were just on sabbatical and eagerly awaiting their next shift!

Until I read this chapter, I hadn't realised how long the old crew have been on shift and until I played with this metaphor, I hadn't realised how slow and heavy the journey has felt at times! Luckily, this chapter and metaphor has helped me to name some of the crew who need a few nights off, and to come up with a plan to work out which elements of my journey might benefit from a bit more planning and support from the right people."

Alexander MacDonald, Lecturer & Career Development Practitioner

A basket of crabs or a pod of dolphins

Did you know that a basket of live crabs doesn't need a lid on it? The crabs will try to escape but, as soon as one is about to make it, the other crabs pull it back into the basket. They are all intent on their own survival and their behaviour prevents other crabs from making it.

Sometimes the idea of us flourishing can be scary for another person – they fear being left behind or their needs not being met. So consciously or unconsciously, they can put barriers in the way. They may dampen your enthusiasm with their negativity, pointing out why making a change would be a bad idea or too risky; they may pull you down by questioning your ability to achieve your goals under the guise of being helpful; they may simply drain your energy for change by placing too many demands on your time and resources. These people are your crabs.

If there was only one crab in the bucket, it would soon climb up the sides and escape. So it might be useful to spot who your crabs are and avoid talking to them about your ideas.

Who feels like a crab (or potential crab) in your basket?
Use emojis to capture expressions that you may see on their faces:

Capture how you feel when you interact with them:

 Describe   Draw  Cut and paste

It can be lonely though to walk (or scuttle) away on our own. Just as we can be drained by other people, we can also be encouraged and inspired. The key is to surround yourself with dolphin people.

Dolphins live in pods but work collaboratively to protect and help each other. They may even intervene to help other species, for example, if a human is in danger of a shark attack. Pods sometimes join together for a short period of time to mate and feed, creating super pods. This expansion helps dolphins to thrive.

Friends of Friends   Community Groups

Self-help Forums   Mentors

Career Coaches

Write the names or draw the people who encourage, support and inspire you.

 Describe Draw  Cut and paste

Use emojis to capture how you feel when you interact with them:

Ask yourself - do I have enough of those kinds of people in my life?
Yes / No

If the answer is No, capture how and where you could find such a pod.

Describe

Larry's reflection upon this chapter:

"We often consider how our experiences shape who we are, but in truth, we know that experience isn't the only actor at play. Our ideas, ambitions and identity are also shaped by those around us. This chapter explores the importance of relationships and the influences of those we surround ourselves with. The chapter has strong links to the research and theory around the importance of other people and our community, in our life and career.

During career development conversations, I have often explored how people act as influencers in a positive or negative way. Using the analogy of 'crabs' and 'dolphins', we can see how the crabs in an individual's life can demotivate or manipulate belief in oneself - sometimes in an unconscious manner. Reflecting on the behaviour of who is around you can involve not only identifying those 'crabs', but crucially the impact they have and how you feel about them.

Many of my conversations with individuals relates to the life and work connections that they have and ones they need to build - considering who can help them manage their career and progress. This chapter forms strong links to this by considering how 'dolphins' provide a circle of support that inspire, motivate and possibly play a mentor role. It also highlights that you can take action, including finding more dolphins."

Larry Hansen, Career Development Practitioner

Managing Your Career

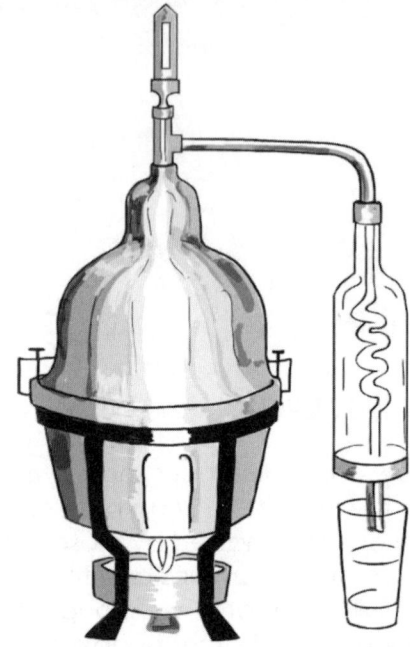

Chapter Titles: read the short statements and see which chapter(s) you are drawn to and sailplane from there.

The river and the stepping stones

When facing any change, it can feel like you are gazing from one side of a riverbank to the other.

Distil your intent!

How would you like to respond when you are introduced to a new acquaintance and asked, 'what do <u>you</u> do'?

Tipping the SCALES ... your hired!

Utilising all six weightings within the SCALES to build a portfolio, which can be used to demonstrate why you are the ideal candidate.

How to TACCL numbers

How often do you use Numbers? Whether or not you categorise yourself as a 'numbers person', numbers surround you. How can they help you in your life-career?

The river and the stepping stones

Metaphors and analogies are powerful ways to bring together the rational conscious part of your brain with the unconscious, intuitive side. They can be used to explore your thoughts, feelings and behaviours more deeply, to gain new perspectives and insights, and inspire you to take action. One that many people seem to find powerful is that of the river and the stepping stones.

When facing any change, you are gazing from one side of a riverbank to the other. The river flows between the banks, and there are stepping-stones to get to the other side. Sometimes the river is more like a stream, the far bank clear and inviting, and the steps across obvious and easy. Other times the far bank is shrouded in mist, the river wide and turbulent, the stepping-stones a bit wobbly and meandering. You have mixed feelings about taking that first step.

Your current riverbank

This is your current situation - what you are doing, as well as your thoughts and feelings about the journey ahead. You may be coming to the end of a course, facing redundancy, in a secure job but feeling unfulfilled, about to retire from paid work. You may be feeling excited, anxious, ambivalent. You may have clear ideas as to what you want to do or the way ahead is shrouded in mist.

What is your riverbank like at the moment? What are you doing? How does it feel? What are your thoughts?

Visualise

On a separate page, create your riverbank, elements could include: size, firmness, sounds, smell, weather?

 Describe   Draw  Cut and paste

Are you on your own or is someone / something with you? What are they saying?

Visualise

Describe

The other side

Do you have a sense of where you want to go? Sometimes a tight idea might restrict you, so we often talk about a broad vision – the type of environment, the tasks you might be doing, the problems you might be solving, the rewards. Some of the other chapters in this book are designed to help you get a clearer vision. You may also be more excited about having a very simple vision, like to find something I enjoy and find meaningful, and be happy taking steps towards it without knowing quite where you may end up.

Imagine that you are suddenly transported to the river bank – you are standing on that ground.

How clear is your vision of 'the other side of the river'? Don't worry if it's shrouded in mist – remember you can keep it very simple.
If you can see the other side (return to your separate page), create what you see, are doing, the sounds, sights and smells.

 Describe   Draw   Cut and paste

Reflection:
- o Is anyone with you?
- o What are they saying?
- o How do you feel being there?
- o Does anything need to change to make it feel right?

Visualise

The river

The river is the journey that needs to be taken to reach your vision. It may be narrow or wide, near or far-away, the waters choppy or calm, fast or slow, sparkling or dark.

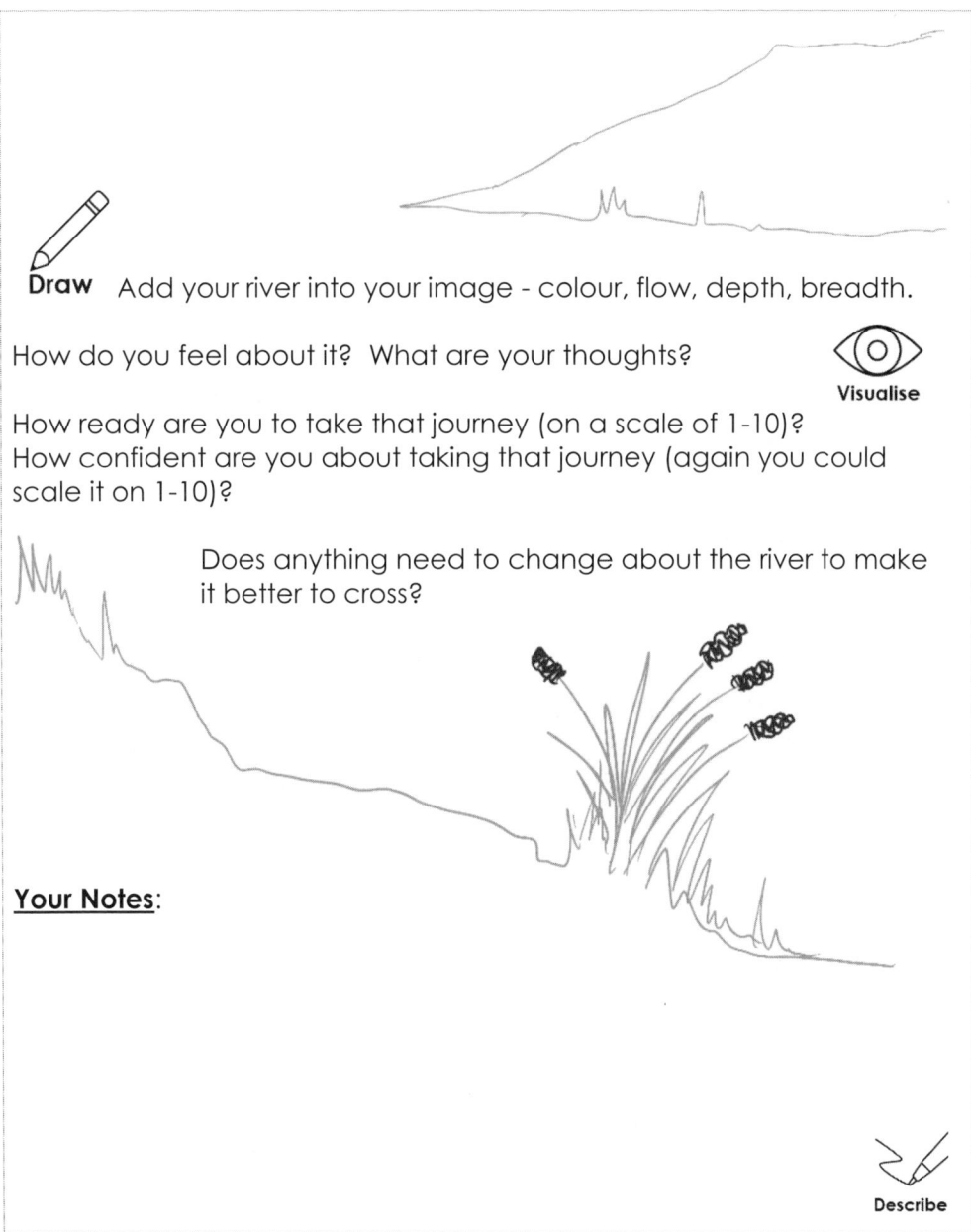

Draw Add your river into your image - colour, flow, depth, breadth.

How do you feel about it? What are your thoughts?

Visualise

How ready are you to take that journey (on a scale of 1-10)?
How confident are you about taking that journey (again you could scale it on 1-10)?

Does anything need to change about the river to make it better to cross?

Your Notes:

Describe

The stepping stones

The traditional image to get across the river is a bridge, but often the journey is not so linear and predictable as that metaphor suggests. The stones may be different sizes, meander, with some tight together, others further apart and requiring a bigger leap (sometimes of faith!). You can pause midway on a larger stone and see that as a good, temporary place to rest. Maybe enjoy the scenery. You may also make sideways moves or turn back and find another pattern. You may be on your own or have others giving you a helping hand.

The stones can be interpreted as the real steps and action you need to take. They can also be regarded as the resources you need for the journey, that you don't need the route all mapped out, but rather concentrate on having the resources to get you there. There has been a lot of research into what people need to effectively navigate the career river – competencies, resources and skills that will help no matter whether you have a clear plan or not, and which allow you to change your mind and direction as and when required.

Have you the resources to cross the river?

In career terms you will need the following ...

- awareness of your transferable skills, values, interests, strengths,
- a broad vision or guiding star of where you want to land,
- resilience and confidence in your ability to undertake the journey (courage when setting out even if you feel anxious),
- a network to support you emotionally and practically, who can open doors to opportunities,
- decisiveness and risk-taking,
- a willingness to tolerate uncertainty, to be curious as to where it may lead,
- research skills to locate the best course and direction to take
- job search and application skills.

How prepared do you feel for the journey? What have you in place and what do you feel you still need?

For a list of the career management proficiencies needed see the river and stepping stones image below.
What do you already have in place? (congratulations – acknowledge your strengths!)

Describe

Which are nearly in place but a bit wobbly/need firming up?

What are the ones that feel too small to stand on/needs some work?

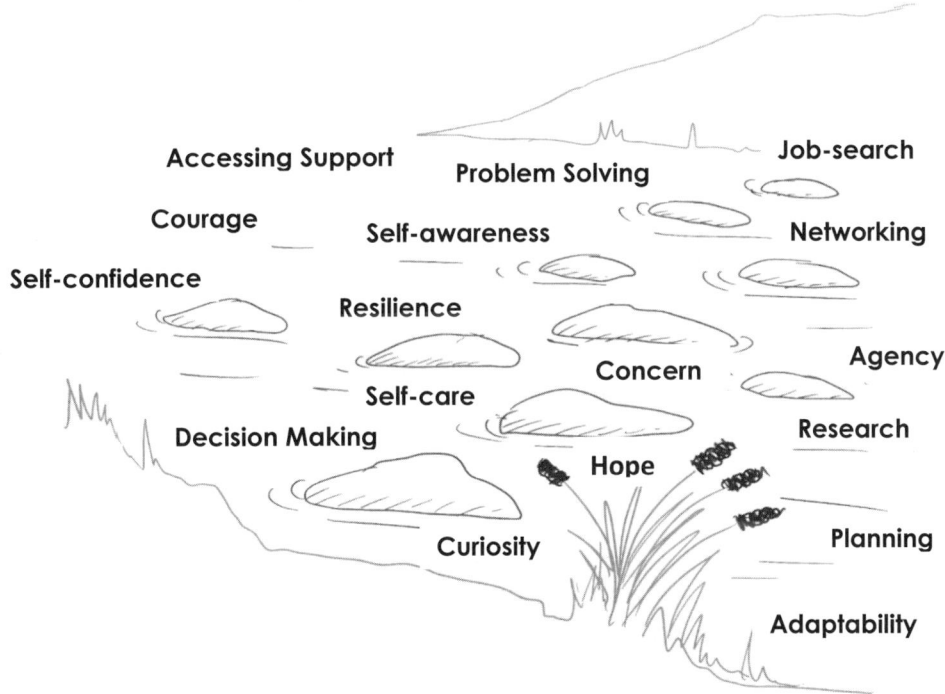

Hang on a bit ...

What if ... some of these skills feel too hard to acquire. Maybe you're thinking it will take years to improve your confidence. Maybe you suffer from depression or anxiety and feeling hopeful is always a struggle. Does that mean that you can't get across? Well that's the benefit of

having stepping stones rather than a bridge – there is always a way across. Some of those stones may be challenges that you carry with you, that can weigh and slow you down, but, like a commando with their rucksack, they also may make you stronger and wiser. You can still get to the other side "in spite of" what's in your rucksack and feel proud of what you accomplished.

Lis' reflections upon this chapter

"My riverbank is shrouded in mist, a little eerie. It's quiet except for the rain. It's a bit muddy, a bit slippery - doesn't feel all that safe. The ground I'm stood on feels uncertain. I might slip. I'm not sure how to move or which direction. Should I turn back into the forest or forge ahead, across the water? The other side looks lush, green, and inviting. It's clear of trees. The sun is shining but it's not too hot. Birds sing and soar. If I were there, I would be standing on firm ground. There would be a pleasant breeze. I would feel calm and free. It would feel like home, with the chance of an exciting adventure ahead.

I don't trust the river one bit. It's passable in theory – trickling, shallow, and clear. But it has been fast and unpredictable. It could change at any moment. I need to be ready. I'm not delighted about the journey ahead. It feels hard. My motivation is low – 4/10, I'd say. Confidence is higher, maybe a 6/10 – if I put my mind to it, I can do it. If I had a wooden bridge, with rails to hold onto, I'd give it a try.

What resources have I got in place that can help me to cross? Well: courage, decision-making. Resilience - check. Concern, determination, and hope seem a bit less solid. Accessing support is barely there, it needs to be bigger to get me across. Could courage and resilience propel me far enough? Or would I need to build motivation and ask for help to get to the other side?"

Lis McGuire, Career Development Practitioner

Distil your intent!

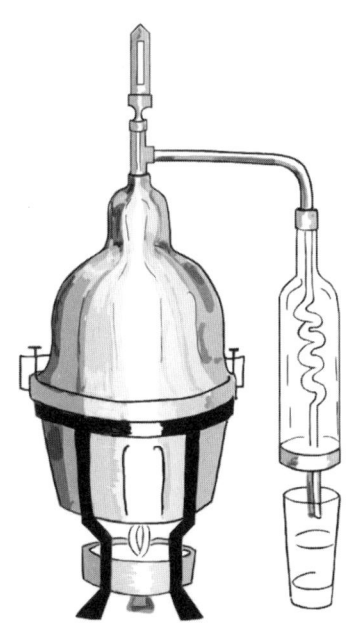

Distillation is an ancient practice, dating back to the Babylonian production of perfume around 1200 BC. Since then it has been applied to various processes of refinement including one of the UK's greatest exports Whisky (including Scotch Whisky). Comprising of three key ingredients: water, yeast, fermented grains (barley, rye or wheat) and aged in wooden casks usually constructed from white oak. It's often regarded as a complex alcoholic beverage due to world-wide regulated classifications: single malt, grain, blended. This means that no two brands of whisky are the same. The most common aspect within the manufacture of all whisky is distillation, where the alcohol created during fermentation is removed from the wash to form a concentrated liquid that goes on to be matured into Whisky. Production of Scotch Whisky has reached 41 bottles shipped around the world every second. In October 2021 a record breaking, single malt whisky sold in Sotheby's in London for $1.9 million. Five hundred years ago the first manufacturers of Whisky could not have predicted that their distillation process and unique blend of ingredients would prove to be a hugely successful world-wide, lucrative business.

You too are a unique blend, of qualities and abilities!

Think about your life and career in terms of flavours, hues of colour, qualities – what would they be?	Describe	Draw	 Cut and paste

Create your own designer label! What font / format would it have: classic, trendy, bold, smooth, retro, regal?

 Describe   Draw

"The purpose of life is a life of purpose",
Robert Byrne

'P urpose' can be defined in different ways for example, an intention or a sense of resolve. Purpose can outline the aims you have in life and your reasons for getting up each morning. Linking a purposeful life to a purposeful career can be viewed as frivolity, but what if more people harboured this intent and strived towards this as an achievement? How might they respond when introduced to a new acquaintance and asked 'what do *you* do', but interpreting this as what is your purpose rather than a job title? The response may include paid employment, but equally could include volunteering, learning or training. If a person has reached or is approaching retirement the question may change to "how do you spend your time", which could include the pursuit of new skills, interests as well as leisure activities. Whatever our age and stage in life, how we fill our days is strongly linked to our identity and sense of purpose.

Imagine you are living a life of purpose, getting up each morning with clear intentions for the day and week.

Complete the table on the next page.

 Visualise

 Describe

Capture how you would spend your time if you were living a life of purpose, what would your days consist of:	Ask a trusted friend or family member to describe what qualities you bring to the world. Capture some points below:

Review both your sections above, circling or highlighting at least three important elements which would contribute to a life of purpose.

Use these important elements to create yourself a future goal (or goals), which captures what matters to you:

Describe

Your intent

The first step towards creating the future you have started to visualise within your goal, is to layout your intention – your determination to act in a certain way.

Create a 'statement of intent', describing what you can do to achieve your goal(s):

Describe

Distil your intent

Negativity or uncertainty could be reflected within a statement of intent by the use of ambiguous words such as: *if, might, could, should, try.*

Similar to the process of distillation, re-drafting your 'statement of intent', by replacing uncertainty with stronger words such as *will, want, know, able*, will purify your intent.

Describe

Complete distillation

Choose one person with whom to share your 'statement of intent'.

This process works best if you read your statement aloud.

As you read your statement, listen to yourself (physical sensations, thoughts and feelings). Capture your responses below:

Describe how you felt when you shared the statement?

Describe

On a scale of 1 – 10, how much do you believe in your future vision (1 being totally unbelievable, 10 being totally believable)?	
If appropriate, once again distil the wording within your statement, strengthening your intent until it feels totally believable.	

Distillation can be continued by you sharing your 'statement of intent' with more people, continuing to refine your statement if necessary.

Luisa's reflections upon this chapter:

"This chapter made me think about how, just like Whisky, we are all individual blends of qualities and abilities. Getting that balance right for each and every one of us can be tricky because sometimes something can happen in the distillation process to upset the flavour ... sometimes it makes the taste bitter or the colour too dark. There could be a blockage in the distillation equipment; the temperature could be too high or too low; there might not be enough air to vent the process.

Life throws things at us! Sometimes unexpectedly. We can all relate to that. We often have to work to get that balance back / get the flavour right for us. Like distillation, landing on our intent might take some time. It may need to be honed and revised.

The record-breaking single malt sold at Sotheby's didn't materialise overnight. Someone worked at it with care, attention, patience and support – to bring it to fruition.

Also, this chapter made me think about how our intent; our wants in life can change over time for a multitude of reasons. In the same way, our palate develops and changes. We might like or not like the taste of a beverage at one point but our tastes can change – as can our intent / purpose at various stages in our life's.

Finally, I love the idea of sharing our statement of intent with someone – almost like sharing a dram!"

Luisa Moreno, Career Development Practitioner & National Executive

Tipping the SCALES ... your hired!

Lord Sugar famously used the statement "You're Hired!" in the final episode of The Apprentice (UK) TV series (The Apprentice, UK, 2005). Candidates jostling for the post of Apprentice faced challenges which tested their skills and character, before being whittled down to the final three. The finalists then faced a rigorous interview process.

Many people find the interview process unpleasant, with anxiety building up beforehand. Knowing that you are going to be weighed up against prerequisites held by the interviewer(s), can feel overwhelming. But what if you could tip the balance in your favour?

In business, time costs money and interviewing candidates can use up a lot of an employer's time. Many employers now use tools, techniques or websites to 'screen out' candidates, thus reducing the number of people called for an interview. At each stage of the 'screen out' process, and when choosing the person to hire, an employer is asking themselves, "*will this person meet the needs of the business / the job role*"? Looking at the selection and interview process from an employer's perspective can prepare you for a more confident display of your employability skills.

The SCALES technique

Utilising all six weightings within the SCALES technique you can start to build a portfolio, which can be used to demonstrate why you are the ideal candidate. SCALES are 6 key employability themes:

Skills – transferable and technical.

Character – values and personality.

Adaptability – responsiveness and managing change.

Learning – knowledge and willingness to learn.

Enterprising – innovative and continuous improvement.

Social intelligence – communication and collaboration.

The six SCALES weightings can be used to guide your research into the company and the job role. SCALES can also help shift your perspective of the recruitment process from candidate to employer. From this viewpoint you will be able to assess what evidence and which proficiencies to use to demonstrate your employability skills, thereby giving you the opportunity to prepare a strong application and perform confidently during an interview.

The power of narrative

The power of narrative is based on one of the most common elements within human interaction – sharing a story. The most effective stories are ones that encourage the listener to imagine the scenario and use their own experiences to create a mental picture (visualise).

Visualise

> Let's test this out ... I was on a family break in the Lake District. The weather was beautiful - sunny and warm. To amuse ourselves we bought a small bright orange dinghy, just big enough for one adult and one child. We wasted no time floating it on the crystal clear, cold water. I thought it sensible to 'test' out the activity, so I waded barefoot into the water. The glare of the sun was reflecting on the water, shining in my eyes. It distracted my attention from the green algae flowing in the water and attached to the rocks under my feet. Even though I shifted my balance as I gingerly lifted one foot towards the middle of the dingy ...
>
> What were you imagining? Did I fall in?

Were you starting to imagine or maybe sense some elements within the story, like feeling the cold water on your feet or the sun shining in your eyes?

A range of well-considered and rehearsed stories are an important tool in your interview arsenal. When shared appropriately and authentically, a great story can have a powerful and positive effect. The interviewer(s) may start imagining you performing the tasks associated with the job role, supporting colleagues, and meeting the aims, ambitions and values of the company.

Weighing the SCALES

The following table breaks down each of the SCALES themes. It provides examples of evidence, a list of potential proficiencies, prompts for your storytelling (context, people, events, actions, outcomes), as well as space to capture your research into the company and job role.

On the following pages, there is space to write down your existing employability skills (what you can contribute to the success of an organisation) or the skills you need to develop against each of the SCALES themes.

Describe

SCALES THEME	PROFICIENCIES	THE COMPANY and JOB ROLE
S – Skills Evidence: • References • Portfolio of activities (for example, photos) • Certificates - qualifications, industry activities. • Narrative (story) – when your skills have contributed to success.	Job specific (job description) Technical Transferable Current Competence Knowledge	
MY EMPLOYABILITY SKILLS		
C – Character Evidence: • References • Volunteering • Interests	Personality Values Ethical (standards) Responsible Reliable	

• Charitable work • Narrative (story) – when you supported a new member of the team.	Motivated Commitment Loyal Confidence Courage		
MY EMPLOYABILITY SKILLS			
A – Adaptive Evidence: • Recognition - nominations, awards • Feedback from colleagues, customers, line managers. • Narrative (story) – when you effectively managed / contributed to change.	Flexible Curiosity Open minded (growth) Prioritising Desire to grow Sense making Critical thinking		
MY EMPLOYABILITY SKILLS			

L – Learning

Evidence:
- Certificates
- Qualifications
- Membership of occupational organisations
- Narrative (story) - describing your learning used in practice.

Questioning
Attentive
Reflective
Solving problems
Self-learning
Inspiring others
Problem recognition
Visualisation

MY EMPLOYABILITY SKILLS

E – Enterprising

Evidence:
- Resources
- Designs
- Projects
- Narrative (story) – when you supported a fresh idea / found a solution.

Innovative
Continuous improvement
Planning for change
Collaborating
Productive
Responsive
Imaginative
Initiative
Creative
Original thinking

MY EMPLOYABILITY SKILLS

| **S – Social intelligence**

Evidence:
• Feedback from colleagues, customers, line managers
• In person - communication
• Verbal & body language
• Rapport building
• Narrative (story) – of how you effectively managed relationships. | Feeling
Communicating
Leading
Collaborating
Integrity
Supportive
Self-control
Constructive
Conflict resolution
Perspectivity
Team player
Self-aware | |

MY EMPLOYABILITY SKILLS

***SCALES* work best when they have been refreshed and aligned to every individual employment opportunity.**

A practitioner's reflection on this chapter:

"This chapter is essential when you need support to take control of the interview process. It will also increase your self-knowledge when connecting to a job role.

You might have lost a clear picture of yourself - where you are now and where you want to be in the future. This chapter is clear, informative and will help you to gain focus. In doing so, this will increase your confidence in identifying the skills and experiences that make you a good candidate for each position that you are applying to.

I particularly like how the 'story element' has been portrayed in the chapter. I believe strongly in the power of visualisation. As a career development practitioner working predominately with adults, I actively encourage individuals to visualise (picture in their minds) the scenarios that they want to share with a potential employer. The importance of evidence-based statements allow an employer also to visualise ('see') you in the role.

These techniques will help you to take control. They will also work effectively if you are supporting individuals 1-1 or working with groups."

Cathy McPhail, Career Development Practitioner

'How To' TACCL Numbers

How often do you use numbers? Whether or not you see yourself as a "numbers person", numbers surround you. From celebrating a birthday, to the time your favourite TV programme starts, you will interact with numbers every day of your life.

You might have heard someone say, "numbers don't lie". Numbers are impartial, neither true nor false, they are clean facts. However the responsibility for the interpretation of numbers lies with everyone.

Numeracy is a language that we all speak. For centuries people have used numbers to communicate in measurements, values or identification. This remains the same today.

When a number is used it provides measurable value, for example, a person says two statements:

- 'I have lots of pets'
- 'I have three pets'

Both are true, but the first statement is vague and expresses the opinion of the speaker, whilst the second statement provides the facts that another person can quantify and visualise.

I was unaware how important numbers were to me, until I wrote a blog about a challenging life experience. Later reflecting on the content, I realised that I used numbers to provide a measurement of triumph over adversity (you can read the blog at the end of this chapter).

Your world, your numbers

Numbers can be found through your life and work stories. They provide a measurement from which another person can draw on their perspective and gain a shared understanding.

There are lots of different numbers that you will regularly interact with example – your bank balance, the time you set your alarm, oven temperature and the number of followers / friends on social media.

Create a list of numbers that relate to your life and work:

Describe

TACCL your numbers

Your numbers are the apparatus needed to confidently manage the recruitment process and navigate challenging interview questions.

TACCL is a framework which can be used to identify the numbers from your life and work which can be used against these five measurements.

TACCL	A measurement of	Numeric example
T: time	durations	I have volunteered with the local youth club for 8 years.
A: achievement	accomplishments	I was in the top 10% of students in my art class.
C: communication	interconnections	I worked within a team of 12 craftspeople undertaking 4 trades.
C: currency	employer values	As an experienced Barista, I have the ability to serve 100 beverages per hour.
L: length	distance travelled	I met the goal of 'couch to 10k' within 3 months by running 4 times per week.

Drawing on your earlier list of numbers that relate to your life or work, create a numeric example for each of the five measurements:

Describe

T: time	
A: achievement	
C: communication	
C: currency	
L: length	

You may find it helpful to discuss your life and work experiences with a friend or colleague, who can help you identify more numbers.

TACCL your numbers regularly, to generate a collection of statements that you can later draw upon.

Numbers and STAR

STAR is a structured method used by many employers to screen in and out candidates. Applicants therefore use this method to lay out their stories in a straightforward manner and demonstrate that they have the necessary skills and experience.

S – Situation

T – Task

A – Action

R – Result

Adding your numbers into a STAR response strengthens the narrative, helps you stand out and provides the interviewer with facts which they can use to measure your ability and consider your suitability for the position.

The blog

October 13th, my son's 2nd birthday. A day planned with fun activities and memorable moments. But before we could commence with the 'merriment' I had to go to hospital to get medical results. I had received 2 letters with different times for the same morning; maybe I should have sensed the urgency, but I wasn't worried; I was more focused on our 12-noon lunchtime trip to McDonalds.

The Ear, Nose and Throat (ENT) clinic was running behind and I was one of the last patients to be taken. David waited with me as long as he could, but our 4-year-old daughter's playgroup finished at 12, so he left to wait in the car, planning to leave if time became too tight. Eventually, I was called into the consulting room to be told that I had Hodgkin's Disease and had to be admitted to hospital after the weekend. I was shocked. I didn't ask any questions. I just agreed to return on Monday and ran out of the hospital to try and catch my hubby.

It's maybe hard to believe but I left the consulting room without knowing I had a form of cancer. When I got home, I phoned my family Doctor. She explained that I had cancer in my lymph nodes and tried to reassure me that the illness was very treatable. Nevertheless, the word "Cancer" terrified me and played on my mind like a broken record stuck on the same revolution. I gathered my thoughts together. I know I had to inform my colleagues at the Careers Centre, but I could not face speaking to anyone, so I contacted the head office and asked them to pass on my news.

I can't say I was feeling at all positive as I went through 3 days of tests, including a bone marrow biopsy. My comments to family and friends are ones which I certainly would not repeat. When the results were ready, I thought I was too, but tumours had spread to the other side of my neck and stomach, so I needed 12 rounds of chemotherapy lasting 6 months.

13th October 2015 is the 20th anniversary of my diagnosis. My son and daughter are nearly 22 and 24, plus it's our 25th wedding anniversary. Lots of numbers, I know, but when you go through a life-threatening situation, every milestone becomes a reason to celebrate.

Some people have said to me that they don't know what to do or say to offer a colleague or loved one support. One of the most helpful *things anyone did for me during my treatment and recovery was saying nothing at all. Being honest and stating that you do not know what to say is OK. I found that I took comfort from someone just sitting with me and listening, even though I was repeating the same concerns which I had voiced the day before, and the day before that.*

There are more and more people overcoming cancer every year. I am happy to report that surviving a diagnosis for over 20 years is becoming more common. Nonetheless, supporting cancer charities and events remain very important, because raising awareness of different conditions and symptoms promotes early diagnosis. This coupled with raising money to fund medical trials and treatments goes a long way to reduce cancer related deaths.

Sally's reflections upon this chapter:

"Reading this chapter caused me to reflect on why numbers are important in my life and career. People often say to me that I am a 'numbers person' but I don't believe I am. If a 'numbers person' is someone good at maths and understands mathematical theories and formulas, well, that's not me. I do not understand financial or balance sheets, theories and formulas completely confuse me, I wasn't great at Maths at School and struggled to pass the exam, but I did enjoy studying it. For me getting the right answer when constructing large tables and getting rows and columns to add up to the same final figure is very satisfying. There is always an answer, it is not subjective and there is always a story behind the figures.

I feel that everyone is a 'numbers <u>and</u> words person' - both are needed to tell the story of your life and career. You will be using numbers daily, but you might not be fully aware of them. The TACCL system enables you to notice valuable experiences throughout your life and career, and to reflect on how to use these numbers within the interview process. The examples should help you consider where numbers exist in your everyday life.

Hopefully you will be able to look back on TACCL and appreciate how understanding this concept has helped you take the next step within your career."

Sally Hamill, Career Development Practitioner & Team Leader

Glideslope into Sailplaning

The connections between our society, the economy and the labour market have become itinerant, stretching, and contracting in direct response to variable market forces. We are in the midst of another industrial revolution where technological advancements, (including artificial intelligence) have once again diversified workforce requirements. The changing nature of "career" is altering the psychological contract between employers, organisations and their employees.

> *"How many people entering the labour market or young people leaving education will experience a 'job for life'?"*

According to the Future of Jobs Report 2020 by the World Economic Forum, half of all employees will need to reskill or upskill by 2025 to keep up with the changing demands of the workplace. This is especially true for young people, who are more likely to enter jobs that are volatile and less secure than those of older generations.

The Shift: Post-modern career

During the early and mid-20th century, career development services supported many young people leaving education with their next steps into roles which matched their skills, qualifications and experience to the opportunities available. Once established within a suitable occupation, this match tended to withstand the test of time. The psychological contract between employer and employees was established. Even though unwritten, it was often expected that, notwithstanding something unexpected occurring, a person would remain with the same employer for a lifetime.

From the mid twentieth century, psychologists, sociologists and economists increasingly turned their attention to applying analytical processes to conceptualise the practice of career-decision making. Each new theory which emerged claimed to "trump" its predecessor by adding an alternative theory of career development, a new dimension to explain career decision-making, (Osipow, 1983). During this era a career was considered to be a linear pathway, where an individual could continue to develop whilst remaining in service to an organisation (Schilling, 2012).

Before the close of the last millennia, post-modern theories began to alert the career guidance profession to a paradigm shift, from linear career progression to individuals having a series of career decisions throughout their lifetime. This contributed to the dismantling of the traditional psychological contract, as fewer employers were able to guarantee long-term employment (Lyons, Schweitzer, Ng, 2015).

During the 1980's and 1990's there was a sharp increase in job insecurity and this brought the concept of tenure back into the political arena. The links between businesses and their workers became tenuous and more short-term. These conditions contributed to a more volatile, commercial working environment. This climate transformed the relationship between individuals and their work organisations, secure employment being traded for overt negotiations detailing mutual dependency. A "new economy" began to emerge based on fundamentally different values and entrepreneurial principles, requiring increased adaptability and innovation from employees and giving rise to the "boundaryless career" (Arthur, Inkson & Pringle, 1999).

Historically, it was quite reasonable for individuals to look ahead and match their future self to an occupation with a stable set of duties and expectations. However, in our current turbulent labour market it is becoming extremely important for young people leaving education and labour market entrants, to develop career management skills in preparation for a lifetime of career adaptability.

> *A 2020 study by the OECD highlighted that Covid-19 intensified the need for young people to develop agency, as well as career aspirations, ahead of their transition from school. (Mann, Denis & Percy, 2020)*

Despite the rhetoric of the new career, literature suggests that many individuals are not prepared for the cultural shift within the modern labour market. To increase the likelihood of success across both life and career, a person-centred approach to career management is required. It is important for career education programmes, parents/carers and organisations supporting individuals, to draw on a range of tools, techniques and approaches to enable individual agency.

The Shift: Protean adaptability

A lack of coherent occupational structure coupled with a diminishing psychological contract between individuals and their employer(s), will undoubtedly construct a new view of an individual's place within the world of work. Constructivism has emerged as a post-modern career development theory (Loven, 2003) which considers the whole person, aligning both life and career, including how individuals derive meaning from their self, environment, abilities, and connections with other people. This holistic philosophy encourages individuals to:
- review their attitudinal response to the modern, unpredictable and sometimes volatile labour market,
- adapt to the environment,
- engage in continuous learning.

The metaphor of water can illustrate the myriad experiences an individual has been known to encounter throughout their life and career. Therefore it is no surprise that the term "protean" has been included within career development theory, (Hall & Associates 1996). Protean is an adjective which comes from, Proteus the god of indefinable weather, a shapeshifter whose versatility gave him control in challenging circumstances. In popular culture "proteus" is a name which has been given to objects or people which adapt in order to operate in specific environments. In each portrayal of "proteus", the ability to change and adapt to an environment is paramount.

Hall examined the protean career in more depth in his 1996 outlandishly entitled book *"Career is Dead-Long Live the Career"*. The title acknowledged the emerging paradigm of The New Career and the requirement to adapt to a new era (Arnold & Jackson, 1997). A protean individual is fundamentally adaptable, possessing the flexibility needed to respond to changing labour market forces. Embracing the protean concept provides a different means to consider an individual as central rather than the organisation.

Some people respond well to change, whilst others avoid it whenever possible. The shift towards the protean concept, where constructing and shaping your own career has become a key life skill, coupled with the necessary development of career management skills, has created an environment which can be more challenging. Social and career structures have been designed in such a way as to place some people at a disadvantage - they are less likely to "fit" and more likely to experience barriers due to access, biased processes and systems, and discrimination. The shift towards increased agency with diminishing employment rights, has placed some people at a greater disadvantage.

In response, post-modern career development practices and service delivery models are evolving to support the development of protean principles of adaptability. These developments have the potential to indirectly drive a successful economy or society, through spirited, curious individuals who are continually assessing what they want and need from a career, alongside developing the knowledge and skills that employers require. We also need to ensure that the profession is actively involved in advocating for inclusive restructuring, challenging bias and discrimination and supporting those who have experienced it.

The Shift: Self-reflection

The ability to adapt within the workplace has always been advantageous and linked to successful careers. Over one hundred years ago, it would have been nay impossible to predict a centenary of technological advancements radically transforming the workplace in the way that they have. Given these changes, self-reflection is required <u>throughout</u> an individual's career to support them to achieve both their immediate career goal and subsequent career transitions. Career assessment tools and activities have long been used to help individuals understand themselves and their skills, for example:

- *Holland Codes (RAISEC) Test (Holland 1959)*
- *Career Beliefs Inventory (Krumboltz, 1991).*
- *Career Maturity Inventory (Crites & Savickas, 1995).*
- *Career Decision Scale (Osipow, et al. 1997).*

The current paradigm shift requires career development activities to incorporate opportunities to reflect on past experiences, the present (here and now), as well as having a future focus, with tangible connections to possibilities. Self-reflection activities have the potential to support an individual to construct, or possibly re-construct their expectations of what transpires within their decision-making processes and throughout their life and career. These activities have the potential to initiate a new attitudinal response and cultivate individual agency.

In order for individuals to exercise their power and navigate this new era of career, some may need to de-construct their existing perception of career as a straight trajectory which ends with retirement (like the cannonball). The concept of Sailplaning has been constructed to nurture self-awareness via temperate curiosity. The activities are aimed at providing individuals with tools, techniques and self-knowledge to sustain fulfilled lives and careers. Navigating an unpredictable 21st century labour market, is something most individuals will encounter on more than one occasion. In addition to the labour market it is important for individuals to also Sailplane through the many other opportunities and environments which life reveals or, at times, can thrust upon them.

Sailplaning aids self-reflection and has the potential to support each person to maintain a life-time voyage of exploration, confident in their ability to navigate, discovering and re-discovering who they are and what is important to them, as their life and career continues to flourish, mature and change.

References

Abadie, M., & Waroquier, L. (2019). Evaluating the Benefits of Conscious and Unconscious Thought in Complex Decision Making. *Policy Insights from the Behavioral and Brain Sciences*, 6(1), 72-78. Found at - https://journals.sagepub.com/doi/full/10.1177/2372732218816998

Arnold, J., Jackson, C. (1997) 'The new career: Issues and challenges', *British Journal of Guidance and Counselling*, 25(4): 427-433.

Arthur, M. B., Inkson, K., Pringle J.K. (1999) *The New Careers: Individual Action & Economic Change*. London: Sage.

Baum, L. F. (1900), The Wonderful Wizard of Oz. Chicago, Illinois: George M. Hill Company.

Chamine, S (2012), *Positive Intelligence*. Austin, TX, USA: Greenleaf Book Group

Crites, J. & Savickas, M. L. (1995) *Career Maturity Inventory*. Boulder, CO, USA: Crites Career Consultants.

Dane, E., Rockmann, K. W., Pratt, M. G. (2012) *When should I trust my gut? Linking domain expertise to intuitive decision-making effectiveness*, in Organizational Behavior and Human Decision Processes, Volume 119, Issue 2, Pages 187-194.

Forrest Gump (1994) Directed by Robert Zemeckis, [DVD]. Los Angeles, CA: Paramount Home Entertainment.

Gardner, H., (1983) *Frames of Mind: The Theory of Multiple Intelligences*. New York: BasicBooks.

Gardner, H., (2006), *Multiple Intelligences: New Horizons in Theory and Practice*. New York: BasicBooks.

Gladwell, M. (2006) *Blink: The Power of Thinking without Thinking*. London: Penguin Books.

Hall, D. T. & Associates (1996) *The Career Is Dead-Long Live The Career*. San Francisco, USA: Jossey-Bass Publishers.

Hambly, L. and Bomford, C. (2019) *Creative Career Coaching, Theory into Practice*. Abingdon: Routledge

Holland, J. L. (1959). A theory of vocational choice. *Journal of Counseling Psychology*, 6, 35–45.

Indiana Jones and the Last Crusade (1989) Directed by Steven Spielberg, [DVD]. Los Angeles, CA: Paramount Home Entertainment.

Jerry Maguire (1996) Directed by C. Crowe, [DVD]. Culver City, CA: Sony Pictures Home Entertainment.

Jung, C. G. (1991). The archetypes and the collective unconscious (2nd Edition). Abingdon: Routledge

Krumboltz, J. D. (1991) *The Career Beliefs Inventory*. Palo Alto, CA, USA: Consulting Psychologists Press.

Loven, A. (2003) 'The Paradigm Shift – Rhetoric or Reality?' *International Journal for Educational and Vocational Guidance,* 3: 123-135.

Lyons, S. T., Schweitzer, L., Ng, E.S.W. (2015) 'How have careers changed? An investigation of changing career patterns across four generations', *Journal of Managerial Psychology* 30(1): 8-21.

Mann, A., Denis, V., & Percy, C. (2020) Career Ready? How schools can better prepare young people for working life in the era of Covid-19. *OECD Education Working Papers No. 241.*

McPhee, J. (1965) *A Sense of Where You Are: Bill Bradley at Princeton.* New York: Farra, Straus and Giroux.

Nightingale, E. (1993) The essence of success: 163 life lessons from the dean of personal development 1993, Nightingale-Conant Corp., Brand: Nightingale-Conant Corp, https://www.nightingale.com/articles/the-river-or-the-goal

Osipow, S. H. (1983) *Theories of career development* (3d ed.). Englewood Cliffs, NJ: Prentice Hall.

Osipow, S. H., Carney, C. G., Winer, J., Yanico, B. & Koschier, M. (1997). *Career Decision Scale.* Odessa, FL, USA: Psychological Assessment Resources.

Pretz, J. E. & Totz, K. S. (2007) *Personality and Individual Differences,* Volume 43, Issue 5, October 2007, Pages 1247-1257. Publisher: Elsevier Date: October 2007 https://www.sciencedirect.com/science/article/abs/pii/S0191886907001225

Robert Byrne Quotes. (n.d.). allauthor.com. Retrieved October 22, 2023, from allauthor.com Web site: https://allauthor.com/quote/12258

Schilling, E. (2012) 'Non-linear careers: desirability and coping'. *Equality, Diversity and Inclusion: An international journal,* 31(8): 725-740.

"Sunday Bulletin Board: `I have dubbed it The Baader-Meinhof Phenomenon'". Twin Cities. 1994-10-16. [Accessed 01/09/2023].

The Apprentice (UK), "The Final, Series 1", created by Mark Burnett, Season 1, Episode 12, Fremantle Ltd, Broadcasted by British Broadcasting Corporation, BBC2, 2005.

UK Government, *The Equality Act 2010.* https://www.gov.uk/guidance/equality-act-2010-guidance. [Accessed 01/08/2023]

United Nations, Department of Economic and Social Affairs, *Sustainable Development, The 17 Goals.* https://sdgs.un.org/goals [Accessed 01/10/2023].

Verbruggen, M., & De Vos, A. (2020). When people don't realize their career desires: Toward a theory of career inaction. *The Academy of Management Review, 45*(2), 376–394. https://doi.org/10.5465/amr.2017.0196

Wizard of Oz (1939) Directed by V. Fleming, [Film]. California, USA: Metro-Goldwyn-Mayer.

World Economic Forum (2020) *Future of Jobs Report 2020.* Cologny/Geneva Switzerland: World Economic Forum.